COMMUNION ON THE ALTAR

STEPHEN OWOLABI

Printed in the United States of America.

For more information, or to book an event, contact :
Email : blog.soundmind@gmail.com

ISBN : 979-899-298-11-0-0

Second Edition: April 2025

CONTENTS

Acknowledgments

A special thank you to Ronda Williams and Oluwatosin Ibiwoye for their invaluable professional input in bringing *Communion on the Altar* to life. Your expertise, guidance, and unwavering support have made all the difference. I am deeply grateful for your contributions to this project.

CHAPTER 1

ENCOUNTERING THE DIVINE: A JOURNEY THROUGH THE ALTAR

There was a closet attached to the room I shared with my siblings while still living with our parents, and during that time I was just beginning to come up in the faith. I was reading books by Professor Zacharias Tanee Fomum about building a consistent fellowship with the Lord on a daily basis. That modest closet became my personal point of contact with the heavens—a small yet powerful space where I experienced divine intimacy. My experiences in those early days of my walk in faith not only shaped the core of my spiritual journey but also formed the bedrock for much of what I have come to experience in my Christian life. They are among the treasures I hope to share through this book.

The altar is more than a mere physical structure; it is a sacred threshold where heaven and earth meet. It serves as the point of connection between the physical and the spiritual. The altar is a place of power, a symbol of covenant, sacrifice, and communion. It is a place of surrender, where humanity offers its brokenness to God, and in return, God responds with grace, mercy, and transformation. To understand the altar is to grasp the heartbeat of biblical worship—a rhythm of giving and receiving, of death and resurrection. Although many people may equate the altar with a physical construct located in a specific place, its true meaning goes far beyond that. When God provided Moses with the instructions on consecrating the priests, He detailed the entire process—highlighting that the altar is not just an object, but a dynamic center of divine encounter.

For example, Exodus 29:35-37 instructs, "Do for Aaron and his sons everything I have commanded you, taking seven days to ordain them. Sacrifice a bull each day as a sin offering to make atonement. Purify the altar by making atonement for it, and anoint it to consecrate it. For seven days make atonement for the altar and consecrate it. Then the altar will be most holy, and whatever touches it will be holy." This passage reveals that the proper consecration of the altar, along with the priests and the tent of meeting, is a meticulous process that ensures everything connected to it becomes holy. Our own righteousness, in contrast, is like filthy rags before the Lord; thus, before any one may approach the throne of divine encounter, a thorough cleansing is required.

The most significant part of Jesus' work on earth was to enter into the holiest of places and to make atonement for all mankind once and for all. His sacrifice transcends any physical table set to represent the altar because He gave Himself completely as the ultimate sacrifice. Through the shedding of His blood, the remission of sins was made possible, fulfilling the ultimate purpose of the altar in a way that no other sacrifice could. Exodus 29:38-42 explains that on a daily basis, a lamb was sacrificed during the morning and evening offerings—a practice that was to continue for generations. This daily rhythm of sacrifice and worship symbolizes the enduring nature of God's covenant with His people.

Sometimes, I wish the altar were merely a place defined by its physical description, but its significance extends far beyond that. For Elijah, who boldly confronted the prophets of Baal, the precise timing of his encounter with heaven was crucial—he approached the altar at the time of the evening sacrifice. For Jacob, the location where he first contacted the power of the heavens was of utmost importance. When he was later asked to return to Bethel—the site of his supernatural encounter—Jacob's journey took on a new dimension. He returned not as the same man, but transformed, greater and more attuned to God's will.

Building a relationship with God, much like any other meaningful relationship, requires mutual commitment from those involved. Our desire to commune with the Lord must be genuine—one that is marked by a heartfelt effort to truly know Him rather than a one-sided pursuit where we use the relationship for our own benefit without considering God's will. In today's fast-paced world, where believers often focus solely on satisfying human needs, there is a risk that the opportunity to build lasting fellowship with the Divine is neglected. Without this intentional connection, a wide gap begins to form—a spiritual gorge that separates us from the fullness of what God intends for our lives.

Many believers, when faced with challenges, simply show up at every mountain and prayer house, hoping that approaching a prophet or pastor will miraculously resolve their issues. While seeking external guidance is not inherently wrong, it pales in comparison to the transformation that occurs when we set aside our fatigue and devote uninterrupted time to the One who truly loves our souls. By intentionally reserving time to commune with Him every day, we take a giant stride toward deepening our relationship with God.

Consider the declaration of Moses when he cried out, "Show me Your face." This was not a casual request, but the yearning of a man who had spent forty days on the mountain on multiple occasions, determined to know God more intimately. Moses understood that if God's presence did not lead the way, then they should not be taken from that sacred place. His words reflect the profound truth that without God, we are nothing.

Similarly, when Paul expressed his desire to know Christ in Philippians 3:13, it was not mere lip service. It was the result of a deep, nurtured communion with God—a relationship that began with that first encounter on the road to Damascus but continued to grow as he experienced more of God's glory and grace. Even if it appears that we have been in a relationship with God for a long time, there is always more to discover, more depth to experience, and a vastness of His glory that we have yet to comprehend fully.

Therefore, I invite us to draw near to God with reverence—a closeness that recognizes Him not as a remote force but as the ever-present One who is intimately involved in our lives. We come with thankful hearts, celebrating the transformative grace that turns our lack into overflowing abundance. We approach with an open, willing spirit, ready to be reshaped and offered up in service, much like the humble bread that is broken and the wine that is poured out. In this communion, the altar transcends its physical form; it becomes a reflection of who we are meant to be—a community of believers molded by God's love and grace. Rather than simply visiting a sacred space, we embody that sanctity, living out our calling with every breath as our lives themselves become the living altar of His glory.

CHAPTER 2

THE BEGINNING: NOAH

We begin the study on altars by looking into their history, starting with the gospel of Matthew. He opens with a genealogy to prove that Jesus is the descendant of both King David and Abraham, just as the Old Testament has testified:

> *"So all the generations from Abraham to David are fourteen generations, and from David until the captivity in Babylon are fourteen generations, and from the captivity in Babylon until the Christ are fourteen generations"* (Matthew 1:17).

During the intervals of these fourteen generations, many altars were intermittently erected and serviced, some of which carried great significance. Altars, we know, took their root at some point and were established to direct our heart to God, starting with Noah.

The story of Noah's life involved not one but two great and tragic floods. First, the world in Noah's day was flooded with evil, and second, it was flooded with water. Of all the people at that time, only Noah remembered God. God's response to this severe, ungodly situation was a hundred-year-long last chance for repentance during which he commissioned Noah to build a graphic illustration of the message of his life. For Noah, obedience was his life; no wonder He was said to be righteous in his generation.

Noah, looking back to the greatness of God in destroying the very works He had created due to their wickedness, must have been puzzled indeed. He surely considered it a wonderful blessing that the same God who was showing him kindness, spared his life and made him an instrument for the continuation of mankind. Thus, when God opened the door of the Ark after the flood, Noah immediately decided to raise an altar in appreciation.

> *"So Noah went out, and his sons, and his wife, and his sons' wives with him. Every animal, every creeping thing, and every bird, and whatever creeps upon the earth, according to their families, went out of the ark. Then Noah built an altar to the LORD, and took of every clean animal and of every clean bird, and offered burnt offerings on the altar"* (Genesis 8:18-20).

Even though Cain and Abel did give offering to the Lord, there is no mention of the word "altar" with reference to their offering. But Noah, who was first mentioned as raising an altar to the Lord, did so after considering the love the Father had for him. *Mizbeach*, which is the Hebrew word for altar was first used in Genesis 8:20 in reference to when Noah built an altar. Altar, as mentioned earlier, is about fellowship. Noah had been growing a relationship with God (Father of all spirits) for about 100 years before this time. He had preached to the people based off of the words he heard from the source to warn them to escape the wrath that was coming. But, as noted earlier, his calls fell on deaf hears. After the words of his prophecy were fulfilled, he decided to raise a physical altar to the one he had had spiritual fellowship with for over hundred years. The physical altar he raised was a manifestation of the spiritual connection he had had with the SOURCE of all spirits for these years.

Noah gave the best of the entire stock of animals. He offered only clean beasts and clean fowls. He could have mixed up the clean with unclean but to further demonstrate his reverence and love for God, and his calling for a relationship rather than just a ritual formality, he gave the best for sacrifice on the altar. God surely would have been delighted by his choosing the best to worship Him.

Noah's actions reflected his heart and love for God which has provided an example for us all. When we want to show our love to God, we must give our best as Noah did. As expected, God felt highly lifted, having seen all that Noah had put into this altar. He drew Noah closer as He smelled the sweet savour from this altar of sacrifice.

> *"And the LORD smelled a soothing aroma. Then the LORD said in his heart, I will never again curse the ground for man's sake"* (Genesis 8:21a).

As a seal of the fellowship that had just occurred between Noah and God, God gave him a sure word of a covenant to convince him of His love which is outlined next:

> *I will not again curse the ground any more for man's sake; for the imagination of man's heart is evil from his youth; neither will I again smite any more everything living, as I have done. While the earth remaineth, seedtime and harvest, and*

cold and heat, and summer and winter, and day and night shall not cease.

Cain on the other hand was looking to show something other than a connection and fellowship with the Source. It's possible he took the step to prove a point to his brother that he was closer to God.

First, Cain was angry when God confronted him about his offering being rejected, fully aware that his intentions were wrong from the outset. He approached God with sin already in his heart, making his offering unacceptable. When the motive behind an offering is flawed, the offering itself becomes meaningless. If his goal was to display a connection with God that did not truly exist, he only worsened the situation.

It is one thing to neglect consistent communication with the Source of Life, but to assume that a mere offering can override a prolonged absence from fellowship is misguided. In contrast, Noah had spent the past 100 years maintaining a relationship with God. This ongoing fellowship made him the right person to establish an altar and seal his communion with the Divine.

Wherefore when he cometh into the world, he saith, Sacrifice and offering thou wouldest not, but a body hast thou prepared me: In burnt offerings and sacrifices for sin thou hast had no pleasure. Then said I, Lo, I come (in the volume of the book it is written of me,) to do thy will, O God. (Hebrews 10:5-7).

Cain's idea was that simply bringing an offering would be enough to please God. However, God desires both the altar and the offering to align as consecrated and acceptable before Him. It is not enough for one to be right while the other is wrong. You cannot approach a holy God with sin and arrogance and expect Him to accept what you present.

Altars and offerings are like male and female—one is incomplete without the other. This truth was lost on Cain. He brought a grudging offering without first establishing an altar. Building an altar requires consistency and commitment; it is not a one-time act. Cain failed to understand the need to submit to the discipline of continually seeking the Lord and building a spiritual foundation before presenting an offering.

In contrast, Abel cultivated a relationship with the Father of all spirits. When the time came to solidify that relationship through his offering, it was accepted because it aligned with God's standards. Through consistent fellowship, Abel learned how God desired to be worshipped. Once he received the revelation of what the offering should be and followed the divine pattern, his sacrifice was found acceptable.

RESULTS OF ESTABLISHED ALTAR

A. Wrath Averted

The story of divine wrath and mercy finds its first turning point in the aftermath of Eden. When Adam and Eve chose rebellion over obedience, their sin rippled through creation, fracturing humanity's harmony with God, one another, and the earth itself. God's response—a curse upon the ground—marked both judgment and a sobering reminder of sin's consequences: "Cursed is the ground for thy sake; in sorrow shalt thou eat of it all the days of thy life" (Genesis 3:17). This decree transformed humanity's stewardship of the earth into a labor of thorns and thistles, a world groaning under the weight of transgression (Romans 8:22). Yet embedded within this curse lay a thread of grace: even in judgment, God's heart leaned toward redemption.

Centuries later, humanity's corruption reached a crescendo. The earth, once declared "very good" (Genesis 1:31), had become a theater of violence and depravity (Genesis 6:11-12). Divine grief overflowed: "The LORD regretted that He had made man on the earth, and He was deeply troubled" (Genesis 6:6). The floodwaters that followed were not merely punishment but purification—a resetting of creation's stained canvas. Amid this cataclysm, Noah emerged as a beacon of faithfulness. For a hundred years, he embodied obedience, constructing the Ark as both a refuge and a prophetic warning. His perseverance stood in stark contrast to Adam's lapse; where the first man succumbed to doubt, Noah "walked with God" (Genesis 6:9).

When the waters receded, Noah's first act was not celebration but worship. He built an altar—the Bible's first recorded *mizbeach* (Hebrew for "altar")—and offered clean animals and birds as burnt sacrifices (Genesis 8:20). This choice carried deep representation. Clean creatures, set apart for sacred use, represented purity in a world still shadowed by sin. The sacrifice's totality—whole animals consumed by fire—signaled complete surrender, a recognition that atonement required the best of what God had spared. The Lord's response was immediate and revelatory: "The LORD smelled a soothing aroma" (Genesis 8:21a). This explains why true worship transcends mere ritual acts. As we can see, God's pleasure arose not from the smoke of Noah's sacrifice but from his consecrated heart—a life poured out in faithful obedience.

In this moment, wrath gave way to covenant. God declared:

> *"I will never again curse the ground for man's sake... Nor will I again destroy every living thing as I have done"* (Genesis 8:21b, d).

This covenant marked a cosmic shift. The Edenic curse, though not revoked, was tempered by mercy. Henceforth, God's patience would anchor the rhythms of seedtime and harvest, cold and heat (Genesis 8:22). The altar, then, became more than a site of sacrifice—it was a bridge between heaven's holiness and humanity's need. Noah's offering reveals a truth that was later revealed in Christ, that ultimate reconciliation would require a perfect sacrifice (Hebrews 9:26).

Noah's altar demonstrates that divine wrath is averted not by human merit but through substitutionary sacrifice. The clean animals prefigured Christ, the "Lamb without blemish" (1 Peter 1:19), whose death would forever satisfy God's justice. Moreover, the covenant with Noah established a template for grace—a promise entrenched in divine initiative rather than human worthiness. Even humanity's inherent sinfulness, acknowledged by God ("the imagination of man's heart is evil from his youth," Genesis 8:21c), could not thwart His redemptive plan.

This account also invites reflection on worship's essence. Noah's altar succeeded where Eden's paradise failed because it aligned with God's terms. Adam sought autonomy; Noah embraced dependence. Cain, later, would repeat Adam's error, offering produce on his own terms (Genesis 4:3-5). But Noah's worship, anchored in revelation and reverence, unlocked heaven's favor. True altars are built not with stones but with surrendered hearts, and God's wrath dissolves in the fragrance of wholehearted obedience.

B. Establishment of Seasons

God's covenant with Noah after the flood extended beyond sparing humanity—it recalibrated creation's rhythms. When the Lord inhaled the "sweet savor" of Noah's sacrifice (Genesis 8:21), His response demonstrated a grace deeper than restraint from judgment: He pledged to anchor the natural order.

> *"While the earth remains, seedtime and harvest, cold and heat, winter and summer, and day and night shall not cease"* (Genesis 8:22).

This promise was radical. After Eden's curse turned cultivation into toil (Genesis 3:17-19), God now guaranteed the earth's fidelity. Seasons would no longer be subject to humanity's failures but tied to God's faithfulness.

Central to this covenant is seedtime and harvest—the twin pillars of survival. Seedtime embodies hope: a buried kernel, vulnerable yet charged with potential. It demands trust, for the sower invests in unseen futures. Harvest, in turn, celebrates fulfillment—the tangible reward of patience and labor. Between them stretches a sacred symbiosis. Without seedtime, there is nothing to reap; without harvest, there is no reason to sow. God's assurance of this cycle is not limited to agriculture—it is a metaphor for His relational faithfulness towards humankind. Just as He sustains crops, He nurtures His promises, ensuring what is planted in faith yields fruit in due season (Ecclesiastes 3:1-2).

Critically, this covenant reflects God's mercy. Post-flood, humanity remained flawed—"every inclination of the human heart is evil from childhood" (Genesis 8:21). Yet God's commitment to seasons reveals His resolve to work with, not against, human frailty. He provides predictable rhythms to support our survival and stewardship. The regularity of planting and reaping became a concrete reminder of His covenant loyalty, a promise that His grace would outlast human waywardness.

Moreover, the seasons dismantle humanity's delusions of self-sufficiency. Farmers may plow and irrigate, but only God facilitates germination. The harvest, then, is both a gift and an invitation—to acknowledge Him as Provider. Jesus later echoed this truth: "Unless a grain of wheat falls into the ground and dies, it remains alone; but if it dies, it bears much fruit" (John 12:24). The death-to-life pattern woven into creation's fabric foreshadowed Christ's resurrection, the ultimate harvest of redemption.

In establishing seasons, God weave His faithfulness into time itself. Each spring whispers Eden's lost abundance; each harvest echoes Noah's altar—an offering of gratitude for a world sustained by grace. The cyclical dance of seed and fruit, cold and warmth, stands as a proof that, though humanity's heart remains prone to rebellion, God's covenants endure, unshaken, and rooted in His unwavering love.

C. Blessing for the Family

God's covenant with Noah reached its crescendo not in restraint— sparing humanity from another flood—but in lavish renewal. After Noah's altar ascended as an evidence of worship, the Lord turned to him and his sons with words that resonated Eden's primal commission:

"Be fruitful, and multiply, and replenish the earth" (Genesis 9:1).

This command was no mere repetition, however. It was a recalibration of grace. Where Adam's mandate had been given in innocence, Noah's was extended to a broken world. The blessing carried the weight of restoration, a divine reset for a humanity still bearing the scars of the flood and the stain of sin.

The Lord's pronouncement overflowed with intentionality. First, He reinstated fruitfulness, a gift that had languished under the shadow of the curse that followed Adam and Eve's disobedience (Genesis 3:16-

19). To "multiply" in a post-flood world was an act of defiance against despair. Noah's family—eight souls stepping onto a barren earth—were entrusted with repopulating a planet still trembling from judgment. God's blessing infused their frailty with purpose: they would become stewards of a reborn creation. Next, the command to *"replenish"* (Hebrew: male—to fill) the earth signaled a return to order. When humanity resists divine boundaries, chaos follows. But for Noah, obedience to this charge would weave stability into the fabric of civilization.

The blessings did not stop there. God expanded humanity's dominion, granting "every moving thing that lives" as food (Genesis 9:3), a stark shift from Eden's vegetarian ideal (Genesis 1:29-30). This provision was both practical and symbolic. Practical, because the earth's ecosystems, ravaged by the flood, required time to regenerate; symbolic, because it acknowledged the fallen state of the human race. Meat, once forbidden, now became a concession to human need—a reminder that God's grace adapts to sustain His creatures even in their brokenness. Yet this permission came with a sacred boundary: the prohibition against consuming blood (Genesis 9:4), a lifeblood reserved for atonement (Leviticus 17:11). Here, God balanced generosity with holiness, ensuring His gifts would not fuel further corruption.

Crucial to this blessing was its communal nature. Noah's family became the nucleus of God's redemptive plan—a microcosm of the "families of the earth" later promised to Abraham (Genesis 12:3).

Their fruitfulness ensured the preservation of the Messianic line, threading hope through generations. The altar, built by one man, secured promises for all mankind. This pattern foreshadowed Christ, whose sacrifice would bless "all nations" (Galatians 3:8).

Noah, flawed yet faithful, became a conduit of renewal. His altar did not merely avert wrath—it unlocked abundance. In a world still groaning under sin (Romans 8:22), God's pledge to Noah tells us that God's covenants are irrevocable, His mercies new every morning (Lamentations 3:22-23), and His blessings, though often entrusted to the few, are destined for the many.

THE NOAHIC COVENANT: WHEN WORSHIP UNLOCKS ETERNAL PROMISES

God's covenant with Noah stands as a monumental promise in Scripture—a divine vow etched not in stone but painted across the heavens. After the floodwaters receded, the Lord declared,

> *"I establish My covenant with you: Never again shall all flesh be cut off by the waters of a flood"* (Genesis 9:11).

To seal this promise, He suspended a rainbow in the clouds, transforming a meteorological phenomenon into a sacramental sign. Unlike later covenants requiring human reciprocity (e.g., circumcision for Abraham, obedience for Moses), this was a unilateral oath. God alone bound Himself, passing symbolically through the "pieces" of a storm-ravaged world, much as He would later walk between divided animals to ratify His pledge to Abraham (Genesis 15:17). The rainbow, then, is more than a reminder—it is a cosmic signature, testifying that God's mercy outshines judgment.

Centuries later, another covenant arose through an act of unbridled worship. When David danced shamelessly before the Ark of the Covenant (2 Samuel 6:14), his critics saw indecorum, but God saw a heart aligned with His purpose. In response, the Lord swore an everlasting dynasty to David:

> *"Your house and your kingdom shall be established forever before you. Your throne shall be established forever"* (2 Samuel 7:16).

This covenant, too, bore the marks of divine initiative. David's abandoned adoration of God positioned him to receive what grace always intended to give. The throne of Israel, though fractured by human failure, became a conduit for the Messiah—the ultimate King foreshadowed in David's line (Luke 1:32-33).

These covenants follow a pattern: wholehearted worship invites divine commitment. Noah's altar and David's dance were acts of worship that unlocked promises far beyond their lifetimes. For Noah, obedience in building the Ark led to a covenant preserving creation itself. For David, exuberant praise secured a lineage culminating in Christ. Their stories dismantle the myth of transactional religion— God desires not performative rituals but relational surrender. As the writer of Hebrews notes,

> *"Without faith it is impossible to please Him"* (Hebrews 11:6).

True worship, like Noah's sacrifices and David's worship, is faith incarnate—a demonstrated belief that God keeps His word.

The challenge is urgent. In an age of distraction, the altar of the heart risks neglect. Yet Scripture urges: *"Bring an offering, and come into His courts"* (Psalm 96:8). Start today. Pour out gratitude like Noah, dance in abandon like David, and watch as worship—raw, real, and relentless—unlocks the unimaginable. For the God who hung His bow in the sky and crowned a shepherd as king still delights to answer surrendered hearts with covenants of light (II Chronicles 21:7, II Samuel 21:17).

Questions for Reflection

1. Noah lived as a righteous man in an evil world. What "evils" do you face at work or other places that challenge your desire to live righteously?

2. Read Ephesians 6:10-17 about dealing with evil. What can you add or change in your Christian walk to be more prepared to live righteously when Satan attacks you through people or circumstances?

3. Think of a time when you chose righteousness while others didn't. What blessings did you experience from God?

4. After the flood was over, Noah built an altar to worship God. Think of a trying time you have come through. How did God help and bless you? Write a prayer of praise and worship to Him:

5. Noah also offered sacrifices at the altar as an act of worship. What can you offer to God? What can you sacrifice for Him even this week as an act of worship for all He has done for you?

CHAPTER 3

ABRAHAMIC ALTARS

God appeared to Abraham one day and promised that his descendants would become a great nation. Abraham's part of the agreement was to obey God. Despite facing severe tests and even an incident that nearly destroyed his family, Abraham remained faithful.

Altars were used in many religions, but for God's people, they were more than places of sacrifice. Altars symbolized communion with God and commemorated notable encounters with Him. One of the most significant experiences I had early in my journey was in the wardrobe of the room I shared with my siblings while we still lived with our parents. Though it was just a small closet—not as spacious as those we see today—it served as a perfect place to avoid distractions and commune with the greatest of all spirits.

In Abraham's day, altars were built from rough stones and earth, and they often stood for years as constant reminders of God's protection and promises. Abraham's life testified that he was a friend of God. He raised these altars as evidence of his close relationship with God, building them for prayer and worship. He could not survive spiritually without regularly renewing his love and loyalty to God; without these altars, he felt lifeless, for they gave him breath.

Building altars helped Abraham remember that God was at the center of his life—a place where he received direction and wisdom about what he ought to do. In a confusing world, having a dedicated space to decompress and rejuvenate is essential. His example reminds us that without a regular commitment to fellowship with the Master, we will struggle to maintain true worship, remembering that we worship not just for what we see, but for what is unseen.

Even though Abraham was childless for a time, he remained committed to the Lord at the altar because he believed in the promise that his descendants would be as numerous as the sand of the sea, even when others could not see it.

SHECHEM'S ALTAR

The first place Abraham raised an altar to the Lord was at Shechem.

> *"Abram passed through the land to the place of Shechem, as far as the terebinth tree of Moreh. And the Canaanites were then in the land. Then the LORD appeared to Abram and said, 'To your descendants, I will give this land.' And there he built an altar to the LORD, who had appeared to him."* (Genesis 12:6-7)

Abraham deeply desired communion with the Lord. No wonder he was called the friend of God:

> *"And the scripture was fulfilled which saith, Abraham believed God, and it was imputed unto him for righteousness: and he was called the Friend of God."* (James 2:23)

His heart was fully set on obeying God. When the Lord instructed him to leave his father's house and journey to an unknown land, Abraham willingly submitted. This posture of surrender and friendship paved the way for him to understand God's voice and follow His direction. When God promised to give the land to his descendants, Abraham's response was immediate—he built an altar to the Lord in gratitude and worship.

Imagine Abraham's thoughts: *What have I done to deserve such a blessing?* The promise of land was not just a personal gift—it represented a greater purpose. Through Abraham, God was beginning His plan to reclaim the earth from the grip of sin and restore it to Himself. Overwhelmed by this revelation, Abraham opened his heart in worship and built an altar at Shechem to honor and thank God.

A Man Called Out of Idolatry

Abraham's family background was rooted in idolatry. Joshua 24:2-3 reveals this truth:

> *"And Joshua said to all the people, 'Thus says the LORD God of Israel: Your fathers, including Terah, the father of Abraham and the father of Nahor, dwelt on the other side of the River in old times; and they served other gods. Then I took your father Abraham from the other side of the River, led him throughout all the land of Canaan, and multiplied his descendants and gave him Isaac.'"*

Despite coming from a pagan culture, Abraham did not embrace the idolatrous practices of his ancestors. Some scholars suggest this may be why God chose him. Regardless of his background, God's hand was clearly upon his life. Even without a religious roadmap, Abraham discovered how to seek and commune with the living God—and he never stopped pursuing Him.

This shows us a vital truth: God values a heart that sincerely seeks Him. Abraham's altar at Shechem was not just a physical structure—it was a testimony of his willingness to worship and follow God in every circumstance.

A Bold Declaration in a Foreign Land

At Shechem, Abraham's act of building an altar was bold and courageous. The land was occupied by the Canaanites, a people who did not follow God and engaged in practices that displeased Him. Yet, Abraham did not shrink back or hide his faith. Instead, he publicly honored God by raising an altar in their midst—a clear declaration that the God who led him was present in the land.

This act could have drawn hostility or even put his life at risk. The Canaanites could have viewed his altar as a challenge to their way of life. Yet, Abraham did not walk in fear. He could have chosen to stay quiet and avoid drawing attention to himself, but he stood firm in his belief that the God who called him would fulfill His promises.

Abraham's altar at Shechem was not just a symbol—it was a spiritual stake in the ground. It demonstrated his faith in God's promise and his commitment to worshiping the Lord openly, even in unfamiliar and potentially dangerous territory.

The Heart Behind the Altar

Abraham's response to God's promise shows us that true worship flows from love, not just obligation. Many people seek God's blessings or turn to Him out of fear, but Abraham's worship was different. He recognized the depth of God's love and chose to follow Him out of gratitude and devotion.

Long before the apostle John wrote the words, Abraham experienced their truth:

"We love Him because He first loved us." (1 John 4:19)

For Abraham, the altar at Shechem marked the beginning of a lifelong journey of worship and obedience. It was a place where his spiritual relationship with God deepened—a place where he acknowledged that everything he had and would ever receive came from the Lord.

Beloved, it is not enough to follow God merely because He is powerful or to seek Him out of fear. True worship is birthed from the recognition of His love and the desire to respond with a heart fully surrendered. Abraham's example calls us to build spiritual altars in our lives—places where we meet with God, express our love, and affirm our trust in His promises.

Just as Abraham's altar at Shechem sealed his covenant with God, our personal altars—whether physical or spiritual—become places where we reaffirm our faith, receive direction, and experience the fullness of His presence.

Abraham recognized the power backing him and refused to compromise his authority in God because of the people around him. He was not intimidated by their presence or fearful of what they might do. With boldness, he established the presence of God over that land.

I challenge you to be bold in your faith as you pursue God's purpose for your life. The altar Abraham built among the Canaanites was a spiritual declaration—an undeniable testimony to the supremacy of his God over every other power that once ruled the atmosphere.

There is no better way to witness the fullness of God's power than by having unwavering confidence in Him. He will meet every challenge and accomplish the impossible. God delights in revealing His greatness, and whenever you, as a believer, acknowledge His supremacy, He moves in extraordinary ways.

CROSSOVER ALTAR

After his first communion with the Lord, Abram was inspired to build another altar. This second altar, known as the "crossover altar" according to Watchman Nee in *Changed Into His Likeness*, symbolized a spiritual transition. It marked Abram's journey from Ai—meaning "the city of ruins"—to Bethel, "the house of God." Abram moved his tent to a place between Bethel and Ai and there, he built an altar and called on the name of the Lord:

> "And there he builded an altar unto the LORD, and called upon the name of the LORD" (Genesis 12:8-9).

Like the worship song by Don Moen, **"Take me deeper, deeper in love with You,"** Abram's heart longed for a deeper connection with God. After his first altar, he quickly built a second one, eager to strengthen his relationship with the Lord. At the first altar, God appeared to him; at the second, Abram called on God by name. His desire was to move from a place of spiritual ruin to a lasting, intimate fellowship with God. As the writer of Hebrews put it, Abram was "looking for a city with foundations, whose builder and maker is God" (Hebrews 11:10).

Yet, even as Abram's communion with God deepened, the adversary was at work. Scripture warns us:

> *"Be sober, be vigilant; because your adversary the devil walks about like a roaring lion, seeking whom he may devour. Resist him, steadfast in the faith..."* (1 Peter 5:8-9).

Satan's strategy is always to divert our hearts from God to worldly concerns. After Abram's encounter at this second altar, the enemy created a test—famine in the land. Instead of seeking God's deliverance, Abram chose to go down to Egypt. This decision led him into fear and compromise. Afraid for his life, he asked Sarah to present herself as his sister rather than his wife. This plan backfired when Pharaoh's officials took her into his household, believing she was unmarried.

> "Then Pharaoh gave Abram many gifts because of her— sheep, oxen, donkeys, men and women slaves, and camels" (Genesis 12:16, NLT).

This was the same man who had boldly raised an altar in a foreign land, declaring God's presence without fear. Yet, faced with danger, his confidence wavered. The lesson here is clear: even after encountering God, we must guard our faith and trust Him completely. Abram's journey reminds us that every spiritual breakthrough will be tested—but God is faithful to deliver those who trust in Him.

Abram's fear of man, rather than trust in God's protection, brought judgment upon Pharaoh and his household. Despite Abram's deception, God intervened for their safety, ensuring that Pharaoh did not retaliate—even after giving Abram many gifts.

> *"And the LORD plagued Pharaoh and his house with great plagues because of Sarai, Abram's wife. And Pharaoh called Abram, and said, 'What is this that thou hast done unto me? Why didst thou not tell me that she was thy wife? Why saidst thou, she is my sister? So i might have taken her to me to wife: now therefore behold thy wife, take her, and go thy way.' And Pharaoh commanded his men concerning him: and they sent him away, and his wife, and all that he had"* (Genesis 12:17-20).

Despite God's promise in **Genesis 12:2** to make Abram great, his faith was still maturing. Beloved, whatever God speaks over your life, He will fulfill. He will also provide the protection necessary to bring His word to pass. It is one thing to fall out of fellowship with God, but it is far worse not to return to Him. This has always been the enemy's desire—from the moment you chose to walk with God. Yet, by God's grace, Abram found his way back.

> *"A fire shall always be burning on the altar; it shall never go out"* (Leviticus 6:13).

Is your altar of communion still burning brightly, or has it grown cold? Perhaps, like Abram, you have drifted toward "Egypt"—a symbol of relying on worldly solutions rather than trusting God. Now is the time to rebuild your connection with the Lord. Even Abram returned to his original altar, where he first called on the name of the Lord.

> *"And he went on his journey from the south as far as Bethel, to the place where his tent had been at the beginning, between Bethel and Ai, to the place of the altar which he had made there at first. And there Abram called on the name of the Lord"* (Genesis 13:3-4).

The enemy is relentless in his pursuit to weaken your faith. He watches closely, waiting for moments of vulnerability—whether through discouragement, disappointment, or delay. When you are weary, he whispers lies to make you question God's promises and doubt His faithfulness. His goal is to create a wedge between you and God, disrupting your spiritual walk and drawing you away from the truth.

This strategy is nothing new. From the Garden of Eden, where he caused Eve to question God's word, to Jesus' temptation in the wilderness, the enemy's tactics remain the same—deception, distraction, and doubt. He knows that if he can shake your faith, he can hinder your purpose and steal your peace.

As believers, we must remain vigilant and steadfast. **1 Peter 5:8** warns us,

> *"Be sober, be vigilant; because your adversary the devil walks about like a roaring lion, seeking whom he may devour."*

Guard your heart through prayer, immerse yourself in God's Word, and stay connected to a community of faith. When trials come, stand firm on God's promises. Remember, the enemy may seek to weaken your faith, but God has equipped you with the power to resist him and remain victorious (James 4:7).

Proclaiming God's greatness does not exempt you from spiritual attack. The devil waits for moments of weakness to strike. As believers, we must guard our hearts and never allow the enemy to disrupt our communion with God—our source of strength.

Though Abram eventually returned to God, he first fell into a deeper struggle. After ten years without a child, Sarai suggested that he take her Egyptian maidservant, Hagar, as a second wife. Abram agreed, and Hagar bore a son named Ishmael. This decision brought long-lasting consequences that continue to affect future generations.

> *"Now Sarai, Abram's wife, had borne him no children. And she had an Egyptian maidservant whose name was Hagar. So Sarai said to Abram, 'see now, the Lord has restrained me from bearing children. Please, go in to my maid; perhaps I shall obtain children by her.' And Abram heeded the voice of Sarai. Then Sarai, Abram's wife, took Hagar her maid, the Egyptian, and gave her to her husband Abram to be his wife, after Abram had dwelt ten years in the land of Canaan"* (Genesis 16:1-3).

Ishmael's birth introduced a conflict that persists today. The angel's prophecy in **Genesis 16:11-12** revealed that Ishmael's descendants would live in constant tension with others, a reality seen throughout history. This conflict arose from a decision rooted in impatience—when Abram and Sarai took matters into their own hands rather than waiting on God's promise. The consequences of that choice continue to affect the world today. This is a reminder that when we step outside of God's timing, our actions can create lasting impacts far beyond what we can foresee.

> *"Behold, you are with child, and you shall bear a son. You shall call his name Ishmael, because the Lord has heard your affliction. He shall be a wild man; his hand shall be against every man, and every man's hand against him. And he shall dwell in the presence of all his brethren"* (Genesis 16:11-12).

Beloved, decisions made in impatience or fear can affect generations to come. The enemy's strategy is to lure you into "Egypt"—away from God's promises—bringing destruction unless God intervenes.

The lesson is clear: **We do not need to manipulate circumstances to fulfill God's promises.** His word will come to pass in His perfect timing. Our task is to wait patiently and trust Him.

> *"For the vision is yet for an appointed time; but at the end it shall speak, and not lie: though it tarry, wait for it; because it will surely come, it will not tarry"* (Habakkuk 2:3).

ALTAR AT HEBRON

It is worth noting that Abram did not just return; he began a consistent walk with the Lord. He settled where the altar had been between

Bethel and Ai. Yet, he did not stop there—his pursuit of a deeper relationship with God led him to move his tent to Hebron.

> *"Then Abram removed his tent and came and dwelt in the plain of Mamre, which is in Hebron, and built there an altar unto the Lord"* (Genesis 13:18).

Having returned from Egypt, Abram recognized not only the pact he had made but also his personal failure to maintain his relationship with the Lord. This covenant was a sacred agreement reflecting God's promise to bless and multiply him (Genesis 12:2-3). However, during his time in Egypt, Abram's actions—such as misleading Pharaoh about Sarai—revealed a lapse in trust and obedience. This realization deepened Abram's resolve to restore his fellowship with God and move forward in faith. This lapse occurred both before and during his time in Egypt. He also realized he had been carrying excess baggage—his nephew, Lot—since he first obeyed God's call. Abram was now determined to rebuild his relationship with God and remove any obstacles standing in the way. Similarly, many believers, when responding to God's call, carry unnecessary burdens that hinder their spiritual progress.

When the opportunity arose, Abram requested that Lot separate from him—not to a nearby location, but to a place in the opposite direction. This echoes the admonition in **Hebrews 12:1**:

> *"Therefore we also, since we are surrounded by so great a cloud of witnesses, let us lay aside every weight, and the sin*

which so easily ensnares us, and let us run with endurance the race that is set before us..."

"And the Lord said to Abram, after Lot had separated from him: 'Lift your eyes now and look from the place where you are—northward, southward, eastward, and westward" (Genesis 13:14).

It appears that a man cannot fully enter into his inheritance until he separates from the burdens that hold him back. For instance, modern believers may carry emotional wounds, unhealthy relationships, or unrepentant sin that weigh them down spiritually. Identifying these burdens through prayer, reflection, and godly counsel allows believers to release them and walk in the fullness of God's promises. Just as Abram's journey advanced after he separated from Lot, so too can a believer's spiritual growth accelerate when unnecessary weights are cast aside. Immediately after Lot's departure, God revealed to Abram the extent of his promised possession. Lot's presence—a man without divine instruction—had delayed Abram's journey. Once free, Abram stepped into a higher level of communion with God at Hebron, a place signifying "firmness" or "solidity." This act deepened Abram's relationship with the Lord.

It is vital to understand that carrying unnecessary burdens will prevent us from ascending to a higher place of communion with God. Abram's decisive step revealed the next phase of his journey—a deeper relationship represented by the altar at Hebron.

"Then Abram removed his tent, and went and dwelt by the terebinth trees of Mamre, which are in Hebron, and built an altar there to the LORD" (Genesis 13:18).

It is through maintaining a consistent, personal altar with the Lord that God's plans for impacting the lives of others through us begin to unfold. When we nurture an intimate relationship with the Creator, our hearts become receptive to His guidance and empowerment. True fulfillment comes not from self-serving pursuits but from serving others as instruments of His love. Without a vibrant connection to the Lord—who continually sends us out on His mission—our calling remains dormant. Abram's steadfast commitment at his altar, refusing to return to Egypt, positioned him to be the man God used to rescue his kin when the time came. His example reminds us that our spiritual station is not about where we are physically, but where our hearts are anchored. Beloved, reflect: are you faithfully maintaining your place of communion with the Lord, or have you drifted to a position where His call no longer reaches you? In staying rooted at your altar, you open the door to divine purpose and the abundant life God desires to manifest through you.

"And He went up on the mountain, and called to Him those He Himself wanted. And they came to Him. Then He appointed twelve, that they might be with Him and that He might send them out to preach" (Mark 3:13-14).

Jesus first called the twelve to be with Him before sending them out. This highlights the necessity of communion before mission. Spiritual stagnancy is a disease, but continual growth in our relationship with God is the cure.

Because of Abram's commitment at the altar at Hebron, God deemed him fit to rescue Lot from powerful kings. With only 318 untrained servants, Abram defeated these mighty forces. His faith had grown to the point where he could confront and overcome great armies.

This mirrors David's journey. His faith, built through intentional worship, enabled him to defeat Goliath. God does not raise His people as the world does. Faith, cultivated through communion, empowers believers to experience divine breakthroughs. Men like Barak, Samson, Jephthah, and David witnessed God's power through steadfast faith.

> *"And what more shall I say? For the time would fail me to tell of Gideon and Barak and Samson and Jephthah, also of David and Samuel and the prophets: who through faith subdued kingdoms, worked righteousness, obtained promises, stopped the mouths of lions, quenched the violence of fire, escaped the edge of the sword, out of weakness were made strong, became valiant in battle, turned to flight the armies of the aliens. Women received their dead raised to life again"* (Hebrews 11:32-35).

Abram's commitment to the altar at Hebron opened the flow of God's promises.

> *"On the same day the Lord made a covenant with Abram, saying, 'To your descendants I have given this land, from the*

river of Egypt to the great river, the River Euphrates" (Genesis 15:18).

God reaffirmed His promises, giving Abram a vision of the future. This covenant was a result of Abram's decision to remain at the place of communion. Commitment to God must be unwavering—following Him one day and turning away the next cannot bring lasting blessings. Abram's life illustrates this truth. Despite his failure in Egypt, he returned to the altar, signifying renewed dedication. This echoes Jesus' teaching in **Luke 9:62**:

> *"No one who puts a hand to the plow and looks back is fit for service in the Kingdom of God."*

Abram's choice to stay at Mamre, the altar at Hebron, led to a divine revelation about his descendants' future.

For any Christian committed to diligently seeking the Lord, the journey can feel like walking on a narrow path filled with obstacles. The enemy uses the world's systems to create distractions and difficulties, making it harder for believers to grow spiritually and fulfill their divine purpose. This is why maintaining an unwavering commitment to God is essential. Without consistent devotion, it becomes easy to drift off course and miss the fullness of God's promises. Just as Abram prioritized his relationship with God by building altars, believers today must cultivate a lifestyle of intentional communion. This commitment not only deepens our spiritual walk but also equips us to overcome life's challenges. When we stay rooted in fellowship with God, we receive divine direction, strength, and the ability to fulfill our calling despite the enemy's schemes.

> *"Then answered Jesus and said unto them, Verily, verily, I say unto you, The Son can do nothing of himself, but what he seeth the Father do: for what things soever he doeth, these also doeth the Son likewise. For the Father loveth the Son, and sheweth him all things that himself doeth: and he will shew him greater works than these, that ye may marvel."* (John 5:19-20 KJV)

Jesus stated that He only does what the Father reveals to Him. Revelation comes from communion with God. Consistent devotion positions us to receive divine direction and protection. **"Give us this day our daily bread"** reflects our need for daily revelation to navigate life's challenges.

> *"The disciples said to him, "Rabbi, the Jews were just now seeking to stone you, and are you going there again?" Jesus answered, "Are there not twelve hours in the day? If anyone walks in the day, he does not stumble, because he sees the light of this world. But if anyone walks in the night, he stumbles, because the light is not in him.""* (John 11:8-10 ESV)

Abram made time to commune with the Lord privately, just as Jesus often did. The phrase "A long while before day" describes Jesus' routine of seeking the Father for guidance. His answer to the disciples' concerns about danger was profound—"If anyone walks in the day, he does not stumble"—meaning that walking under divine revelation ensures safety. Revelation remains the key to a victorious life.

MOUNT MORIAH
THE ULTIMATE ALTAR

As arrows are expertly crafted to fly true and hit their intended target, so too is every child born destined to impact the world. Each life, like a well-aimed arrow, finds its mark along the journey. This truth is vividly illustrated in the life of Abraham, who emerged as an example for all men. Through his unfolding journey and the various stages of the altar, Abraham demonstrated the need for continual growth in faith, leading others into an everlasting fellowship with their Creator.

> *"Children are a gift from the LORD; they are a reward from him. Children born to a young man are like arrows in a warrior's hands"* (Psalm 127:3-4, NLT).

It is important to note that the man known as Abram encountered God in a search for divine truth. To seal this revelation of his heavenly Father, God bestowed upon him a new name—he was no longer "Abram" but became "Abraham." This renaming signified that no one can approach the Lord except as He grants. Drawn closer by God's loving hand, Abraham set his heart on reaching the highest level of communion, which would culminate at Mount Moriah. His journey had taken him from the altar at Hebron, where he had once worshiped, toward a new horizon. In fact, Abraham had even risen from his altar at Hebron and moved south to dwell among the Philistines (Genesis 20:1).

God guided Abraham along this path to demonstrate the transformative work He had accomplished in the life of a man who had remained steadfast at the communion altar. Abraham's unyielding faith instilled fear even in the heart of Abimelech, the king of the Philistines at that time. Today, many believers lead a defensive life—constantly praying and trying to dodge or repel every arrow that the enemy fires. However, Abraham operated beyond mere peripheral knowledge of God. He was bold and unafraid; his presence in any domain caused kings and their subjects alike to tremble, for God's hand was unmistakably upon him.

As children of the kingdom, we are called to live not as those who have no true relationship with God, but as people who fully embrace the One who governs the affairs of all men. It is essential to cast off a mindset of spiritual bondage—the kind that portrays us as if our Heavenly Father were imprisoned behind bars. Such a mindset grieves God, for it fails to reflect the freedom and boldness that Abraham so fearlessly displayed. When others observe the way Abraham shut down kings who dared stand in his path, they are witnessing the power of a life wholly devoted to the Lord. Until we begin to think and act like children of the kingdom, the enemy will always seek to caricature our faith.

When Abimelech and Phichol, the chief captain of his host, witnessed the respect and authority that Abraham commanded due to his unwavering covenant with God, they approached him for a covenant of their own. They were fearful that Abraham might soon become too powerful to control. Rather than risking being subjugated when he grew even stronger, they desired to become allies and share in the blessing of God's hand upon Abraham's life.

> *"And it came to pass that Abimelech and Phichol spoke unto Abraham, saying, "God is with thee in all that thou doest: now therefore swear unto me by God that thou wilt not deal falsely with me, nor with my son, nor with my son's son; but according to the kindness that I have done unto thee, thou shalt do unto me, and to the land wherein thou hast sojourned""* (Genesis 21:22-23).

> *"Thus, a covenant was made at Beersheba; thereafter, Abimelech and Phichol returned to the land of the Philistines. Meanwhile, Abraham planted a grove in Beersheba and called upon the name of the LORD on Philistine soil for many days"* (Genesis 21:32-34).

While Abraham was still reveling in the newfound glory of his covenant with Abimelech, God summoned him to the **Ultimate of All Altars**. Beloved, we are engaged in a spiritual marathon—not a sprint—with our God. All He desires is our unwavering commitment, and that is precisely what the enemy covets. Ultimately, it comes down to our choice to remain with the Father of all spirits by maintaining constant communion at the altar.

A brother once shared his conversion story with me. He recalled that when he first came to Christ, nothing seemed to change because his life had always been good. But for Abraham, everything transformed. His very identity was remade—his name was changed, and he became the father of nations, no longer merely a father. Abraham's willingness to give all at the altar of sacrifice without a hint of complaint sealed his relationship with his Lord. He willingly sacrificed what was required, even cutting short his sojourn in Egypt, so that he could remain devoted to God.

Yet, God's plan for Abraham was far from complete. Determined to lead him into the ultimate communion with Himself, God then asked for something no less than His Only Son.

> *"Then he said, 'Take now your son, your only son Isaac, whom you love, and go to the land of Moriah, and offer him there as a burnt offering on one of the mountains of which I shall tell you'"* (Genesis 22:2, NKJV).

This command might seem perplexing, especially since Ishmael was Abraham's firstborn. However, by the terms of the covenant, Isaac was the only son through whom the promise would be fulfilled. At this point, Abraham no longer knew the whereabouts of Ishmael, having released him and his mother to go their own way (Genesis 21:9-12).

God instructed Abraham to build an altar on Mount Moriah. With a heavy heart, Abraham bound his beloved son and prepared to offer him as a sacrifice. At the critical moment, when Abraham was about to carry out the unthinkable, the angel of the Lord intervened and instructed him to stop, for God had provided a lamb for the sacrifice. In that miraculous moment, Abraham named the place JEHOVAH JIREH ("The LORD Will Provide," Genesis 22:14).

This event marked the pinnacle of the altars in Abraham's journey. After this divine encounter, Abraham remained in the highest level of communion with God, no longer needing to offer animal sacrifices. This pivotal moment points us to the promise of a new covenant, as prophesied by Jeremiah:

> *"Behold, the days come," saith the LORD, "that I will make a new covenant with the house of Israel, and with the house of Judah... I will put my law in their inward parts, and write it in their hearts; and will be their God, and they shall be my people"* (Jeremiah 31:31-34).

The depth of communion with the Lord is never without cost. Abraham's willingness to sacrifice his son foreshadowed the ultimate redemption—God redeeming humanity through the sacrifice of His own Son, Jesus Christ. If your journey with the Lord has not been marked by sacrifices and the scars of holy loss, it may be time to call upon Him for a renewed walk. Often, the burdens we let go of leave scars that testify to the transformative power of the altar.

In the end, every communion with the Lord that demands sacrifice and leaves its mark is a sign of true redemption. Just as Abraham's faith was tested and refined on Mount Moriah, so too are we called to allow our lives to be molded by the altar of communion. Only then can we fully experience the promise of a renewed covenant with God.

Questions for Reflection

1. Abraham pursued a relationship with God. In what ways are you seeking Him?

2. The enemy led Abraham away from his Lord. How can you better prepare yourself to recognize Satan's schemes and resist him?

3. Abraham and Sarah did not wait on the Lord to bring them a son. When have you gone ahead of God's timing? What did you learn? Were you or others hurt by your impatience? What would you have done differently?

4. Where and when do you spend time alone with the Lord? What do you daily do to try and build your relationship with Him?

5. Abraham was willing to offer God his ultimate sacrifice and obedience. What is God calling you to sacrifice? What is He calling you to obey?

CHAPTER 4

DAVIDIC ALTARS

In the course of my personal study of 2 Chronicles, I reached the third chapter and discovered that the temple was built at the very place where David also offered his sacrifice to the Lord on the threshing floor of Ornan. I further learned that Mount Moriah—where Abraham was prepared to sacrifice Isaac before the angel of the Lord intervened—is located in the same vicinity. I believe this was not mere coincidence but part of God's master plan.

The revelatory experience of encountering God at the altar of worship reached a significant milestone for Abraham at Mount Moriah. Yet this was not the ultimate peak for all ages. Today, we observe a new level of communion with God, one that emerged after fourteen generations. Beloved, there is no limit to the depth of understanding we can experience with the God we walk with. The worship lives of Isaac—and later Jacob, Abraham's son and grandson respectively—reflected an even greater depth of covenantal relationship than their forefather had known. To Isaac, God declared:

> *"And I will make thy seed to multiply as the stars of heaven, and will give unto thy seed all these countries; and in thy seed shall all the nations of the earth be blessed; Because that Abraham obeyed my voice, and kept my charge, my*

commandments, my statutes, and my laws" (Genesis 26:4).

And to Jacob, God revealed in a dream:

> *"And he dreamed, and behold a ladder set up on the earth, and the top of it reached to heaven: and behold, the angels of God ascending and descending on it. And, behold, the LORD stood above it, and said, I am the LORD God of Abraham thy father, and the God of Isaac: the land whereon thou liest, to thee will I give it, and to thy seed; And thy seed shall be as the dust of the earth, and thou shalt spread abroad to the west, and to the east, and to the north, and to the south: and in thee and in thy seed shall all the families of the earth be blessed. And, behold, I am with thee, and will keep thee in all places whither thou goest, and will bring thee again into this land; for I will not leave thee, until I have done that which I have spoken to thee of"* (Genesis 28:12-15).

In these encounters, God interrupted the course of their lives to reveal His plan and direction. God is always on the move; what He did yesterday is not a yardstick for understanding or defining His future movement. He has remembered His covenant forever—the command He gave to a thousand generations. "Which covenant He made with Abraham, and His oath unto Isaac; And confirmed the same unto Jacob for a law, and to Israel for an everlasting covenant" (Psalms 105:8-10).

The transition of this covenant from Abraham, through Isaac, to Jacob—and even extending to a thousand generations—reveals how dynamic God is. As Christians, we often think that these established rules and traditions in worship are unchanging, and we cling to them, sometimes even resisting necessary change. Yet we forget that God Himself might move us to leave behind the monuments we have built for Him. Worship at the altar is dynamic, and only the Holy Spirit can free us from rigid, outdated routines. God is ever-changing, so open your eyes, ears, and heart to the Holy Spirit, that He might speak to you at the altar for His glory and that you might experience His holy presence. When Abraham's descendants found themselves uncertain about which path to follow, the altar of covenant and worship always provided clear direction.

Consider the account of Jacob when he was told, "Joseph is yet alive, and he is governor over all the land of Egypt." His heart fainted, and he hardly believed the words until he saw the wagons Joseph had sent. In that moment, Jacob's spirit was revived, and he declared, "It is enough; Joseph my son is yet alive: I will go and see him before I die" (Genesis 45:26-28). Later, as Israel journeyed to Beersheba, he offered sacrifices to the God of his father Isaac. During the night, God spoke to Israel in visions, saying, "Jacob, Jacob." And when Jacob answered, God said, "I am God, the God of your father; do not be afraid to go down into Egypt, for I will make you a great nation there. I will go down with you into Egypt, and I will certainly bring you up again; and Joseph shall put his hand upon your eyes." Thus, Jacob rose from Beersheba, and his sons carried him, along with his family and belongings, into Egypt (Genesis 46:1-6).

It is intriguing that while God instructed Isaac not to go down to Egypt

(Genesis 26:2), He later directed Jacob to go there. This contrast reminds us that God's methods are dynamic and cannot be confined to the monuments we construct as symbols of our faith. The altars of worship provided the direction Jacob needed, ultimately leading his descendants into becoming a sovereign nation.

Beloved, regardless of how uncertain the future may seem, a consistent act of worship in the sanctuary elevates you into God's divine plan—one that will always exceed your wildest imaginations. When we maintain our communion with God at the altar, we position ourselves to receive His guidance and partake in His blessings. Even as the covenant transitions from one generation to the next, the call to deeper worship remains constant.

The altars of the Davidic era, established by our forefathers, serve as a powerful reminder of this dynamic relationship. They reveal that the true essence of worship is not static but ever-evolving. As we encounter God in worship, our hearts are transformed, and we are enabled to impact the world around us in profound ways. The worship of Isaac, and later Jacob, reflected an evolving covenant—a walk that not only built on the foundation laid by Abraham but also expanded its promise to every nation and generation that followed.

In our own lives, we must be willing to let go of the old and embrace the new dimensions of worship that God reveals to us. The dynamic nature of the covenant means that God's plan for our lives can transform and grow in ways we might never expect. It calls us to be open to His leading, to let the Holy Spirit renew our hearts continuously, and to prepare ourselves to receive new revelations at the altar of communion.

Indeed, as we look back on the altars of our spiritual heritage, from Abraham to Isaac to Jacob, we see a clear trajectory of growth and divine intimacy. These sacred spaces were not merely places of ritual but were the very settings where God's promises were reinforced and His plans unfolded. They were the places where doubts were dispelled and where the assurance of God's everlasting covenant was made manifest.

So let us examine our own lives: Are we willing to step into the dynamic worship that God calls us to? Do we allow the altars of our hearts to be cleansed and renewed continuously, making room for His ever-new revelation? It is in that sacred space of communion that God's purposes for us are revealed, and our lives become instruments for His glory, just as it was for the heroes of faith before us.

TRANSITION FROM ABRAHAMIC TO DAVIDIC ALTARS
MOSAIC ALTAR

Moses arose as the deliverer for the children of Israel, descending from his great-grandfather Levi, to liberate a people who had multiplied greatly and were destined to worship the one true God. In bondage, they had no time or place to enjoy true communion at the altar. God heard their anguished cries and sought a man willing to submit to His guidance so that the children of Israel might be freed and restored to worship at the altar of sacrifice.

When anything or anyone deprives a believer of the precious time to worship God, He is deeply displeased and will act with determination—bringing calamity upon that thing or person. We witnessed this when Pharaoh kept the children of Israel in slavery, refusing to let them go. In response, God raised Moses to confront Pharaoh and dismantle his oppressive reign over His people.

> *"Let us hear the conclusion of the whole matter: Fear God, and keep His commandments: for this is the whole duty of man"* (Ecclesiastes 12:13).

Fear God. Today, apart from the remnants of physical slavery—which modern civilized societies now reject—certain corporate organizations continue to function like altars, linking our world system to demonic influences. Their modus operandi mirrors slavery, showing no regard for our inherent humanity.

As Proverbs 6:26 warns,

> *"For by means of a whorish woman a man is brought to a piece of bread: and the adulteress will hunt for the precious life."*

Demonic forces, acting as agents of bondage, seek attention and worship and, in doing so, use human beings as their altars. They appear in various guises, sometimes masquerading as the so-called children of God. Although their outward appearance may seem innocent, their inner nature is dangerous. Beloved, our bodies are the temple of the Holy Spirit; no other being or influence should ever be permitted to dwell within them.

THE PASSOVER

The Passover brought about the total liberation of the people of God from slavery, freeing them to become the warriors of worship they were meant to be. This victory was not achieved without God establishing judgment upon the altars of the Egyptians to display His supremacy over their false gods. He elevated Israel into a higher spiritual walk within His covenant by instituting a system of priests, ensuring that sacrifices were offered continuously—morning and evening—and that the fire on the altar was never allowed to be extinguished.

> *"And the fire upon the altar shall be burning in it; it shall not be put out: and the priest shall burn wood on it every morning, and lay the burnt offering in order upon it; and he shall burn thereon the fat of the peace offerings. A fire shall ever be burning upon the altar; it shall never go out"* (Leviticus 6:12-13).

Furthermore, the LORD commanded,

> *"And thou shalt command the children of Israel, that they bring thee pure oil beaten for the light, to cause the lamp to burn always. In the tabernacle of the congregation without the vail, which is before the testimony, Aaron and his sons shall order it from evening until morning before the LORD: it shall be a statute forever unto their generations on the behalf of the children of Israel"* (Exodus 27:20-21).

Prior to this period, altars were serviced only on demand (as seen in

Genesis 22 and Genesis 46). However, a continuous fire upon the altar of sacrifice was instituted, and certain individuals were set apart for this sacred task. Initially, the firstborn son of each family served this purpose (Exodus 13:12), but eventually, the Levites were chosen. The LORD spoke to Moses, saying,

> *"Bring the tribe of Levi near, and present them before Aaron the priest, that they may serve him. And they shall attend to his needs and the needs of the whole congregation before the tabernacle of the meeting, to do the work of the tabernacle. Also they shall attend to all the furnishings of the tabernacle of meeting, and to the needs of the children of Israel, to do the work of the tabernacle. And you shall give the Levites to Aaron and his sons; they are given entirely to him from among the children of Israel. So you shall appoint Aaron and his sons, and they shall attend to their priesthood; but the outsider who comes near shall be put to death."*

Then the LORD spoke to Moses, saying,

> *"Now behold, I Myself have taken the Levites from among the children of Israel instead of every firstborn who opens the womb among the children of Israel. Therefore the Levites shall be mine"* (Numbers 3:5-12).

The sanctity that God attached to worship on the altar compelled Him to set apart the tribe of Levi so that they might minister to the priest who, in turn, ministered to the LORD. Strangers—those who had not been circumcised and saved—were not permitted to partake in this worship.

The act of worship and the remembrance of our covenant relationship with the LORD should not be confined merely to moments of crisis or when we are in dire need of a divine word; rather, it ought to be a continual service offered to the LORD—at home, in the office, and in every place where we have the privilege to encounter Him. Moses was instrumental in ensuring that the children of Israel experienced a continuous pattern of worship, establishing both the ordinance and the guiding law for their lives.

That first covenant between God and Israel contained regulations for worship and prescribed a place of worship here on earth. The Tabernacle was divided into two rooms. The first, known as the Holy Place, housed a lampstand, a table, and sacred loaves of bread. Beyond a curtain lay the second room, the Most Holy Place, where a golden incense altar and the Ark of the Covenant—a wooden chest overlaid with gold on all sides—were kept. Within the Ark were contained a golden jar of manna, Aaron's staff that had budded, and the stone tablets of the covenant. Over the Ark, cherubim of divine glory stretched their wings over the cover, the place of atonement. While we cannot detail these sacred items further now, it is important to note that once everything was in place, the priests regularly entered the Holy Place to perform their duties, though only the high priest was permitted to enter the Most Holy Place—and that too only once a year, when he offered blood for his own sins and for the sins of the people, who had sinned unknowingly (Hebrews 9:1-7, NLT).

The mosaic level of worship initiated a movement toward the sanctity that the body of God's children should possess. Order was introduced, and a day was set aside for divine worship unto the Most High who had rescued their lives. No longer were they merely a wandering, downtrodden people; they had been set apart.

With the opening of the covenant and the maintenance of daily worship and sacrifice, the presence of God became increasingly manifest among His people. He spoke through Moses, through the mountains and clouds, and His presence grew visible. His ordinances were obeyed with greater devotion, for any attempt to break these commandments was met with the fierce judgment of the LORD, who is the consuming fire and responds with a roar of judgment. Disaster, in the form of death, pestilence, and other terrifying calamities, accompanied His wrath.

Moses, the man who instituted a genuine, law-based worship experience, left the people with these final instructions as his departure drew near:

> *"These are the statutes and judgments, which you shall be careful to observe in the land which the LORD God of your fathers is giving you to possess, all the days that you live on the earth. You shall utterly destroy all the places where the nations which you shall dispossess served their gods, on the high mountains and on the hills and under every green tree. And you shall destroy their altars, break their sacred pillars, and burn their wooden images with fire; you shall cut down the carved images of their gods and destroy their names from that place. You shall not worship the LORD your God with*

such things. But you shall seek the place where the LORD your God chooses, out of all your tribes, to put His name for His dwelling place; and there you shall go. There you shall take your burnt offerings, your sacrifices, your tithes, the heave offerings of your hand, your vowed offerings, your freewill offerings, and the firstborn of your herds and flocks" (Deuteronomy 12:1-6).

Moses commanded that the Israelites destroy all the altars of the gods of the lands they were about to enter so that the memory of those false gods would be eradicated from Israel. God understood that if the Israelites left behind these monuments, they might easily be tempted to revert to worshiping the gods of those lands.

We do not own our lives, and the fact that a particular style of worship in a given center might appeal to our emotions does not make it right. It might satisfy our senses, but any form of worship that deviates from the throne of God will incur His wrath rather than His blessing—just as when Nadab and Abihu, the sons of Aaron, offered "strange fire" before the LORD.

> *"And Nadab and Abihu, the sons of Aaron, took either of them his censer, and put fire therein, and put incense thereon, and offered strange fire before the LORD, which He commanded them not. And there went out fire from the LORD, and devoured them, and they died before the LORD"* (Leviticus 10:1-2).

The attachments we hold onto from our worldly life—if not cast aside—will ultimately lead to our downfall. We must confess our sins before the LORD, repent, and seek His forgiveness. "There is therefore now no condemnation to them which are in Christ Jesus, who walk not after the flesh, but after the Spirit" (Romans 8:1).

Having left behind those weights, what is our next step? "Walk in the Spirit and you shall not fulfill the lust of the flesh" (Galatians 5:16).

We can only worship God in truth and in spirit through our Lord and Savior, Jesus Christ, who guides us in worship. The truth is that as we choose to worship God alone, we must relinquish all other powers. In response, God will move to perform amazing works in and around our lives—works beyond our comprehension.

THE MOSAIC ALTAR INTERPRETED

(This entire section is authored by Martyn Barrow and used by permission.)

The Golden Incense Altar was made of acacia wood overlaid with gold. It was situated just in front of the Veil, the curtain which separated the Holy Place from the Holy of Holies. It was square: half a metre by half a metre wide, and one metre high. The priest had to burn incense at this altar in the morning and at twilight (Exodus 30:7-8) as a perpetual fragrance before the Lord. The burning incense signifies prayer (Psalm 141:2, Revelation 5:8) and points us to the prayer of the Lord Jesus in the garden of Gethsemane (John 17, Mark 14:42).

Similar to the Showbread Table, the Golden Incense Altar had a golden crown round the top of it. This signifies "Jesus, crowned with glory and honour" (Hebrews 2:9) However, because the Golden Incense Altar is the place of prayer, the crown and the prayer together give us a hint of a kingly priesthood. This thought is developed in the book of Hebrews: the Messiah, Jesus Christ has become a priest according to the Lord. Melchizedek (Psalms. 110:1, Hebrew 7). He can sympathize with us as our High Priest (Hebrew 4:15) and He is able to minister His supply of mercy and grace to us as the King of righteousness a King of peace (Hebrews: 25, 2; 4:16 Genesis 14:18).

Prayer is very important in the daily life of all believers in the Lord (Daniels 10 Matthews 6:5-13). We should **"pray without ceasing"** (1 Thessalonians 5:17), using all kinds of prayers and petitions with thanksgiving, praying at every time in the Spirit, watching and persevering in prayer not just for ourselves but for all our brothers and sisters (Ephesians 6:18). Prayer is becoming increasingly important, especially as the battle intensifies and utterance of the gospel becomes harder (Ephesians 6:19). However, when our prayer is genuinely at the Golden Incense Altar, the Lord causes much incense to be added to our prayer.

That incense rises back to Him as we pray according to His will, and the results are dramatic (Revelation 8:3-4). The Tabernacle is the house of God, His dwelling place (Exodus 25:8-9) and a fore shadow of both Christ and the Church (Colossians 2:9; I Timothy 3:15; Ephesians 2:21-22). It is God's desire that His house should be a house or prayer for all nations (Isaiah 56:7).

For us to pray at the Golden Incense Altar, blood must first be applied

(Leviticus 4:7), the blood of the Sin Offering. Then the incense must be prepared with genuine acknowledgments and experiences of the Son's Name—His purity, holiness, subjection, faith and dependence on God the Father.

> *"And in that day you will ask Me nothing. Most assuredly, I say to you, whatever you ask the Father in My name He will give you. Until now you have asked nothing in My name. Ask, and you will receive, that your joy may be full"* (John 16:23-24, NKJV).

One of the ingredients of the incense was salt, to make our prayer neither sentimental nor formal. We should pray at every time in the Spirit (Ephesians 6:18) in the Son's Name. This will be sweet to God the Father. Jesus's ministry was not just healing and teaching people; it was also a service to God the Father in His living and in praying (Mark 1:32-35). The night before He chose His twelve disciples, Jesus spent the whole night in the prayer "that you may not enter into temptation" and His observation regarding praying that **"the spirit is willing, but the flesh is weak"** (Matthew 26:41). These so obviously come from One who is qualified to comment (Hebrews 2:14, 18).

There in the garden of Gethsemane, Jesus is at the Golden Incense Altar on the night before the Veil (that is His flesh, Hebrews 10:20) which would be torn from top to bottom by God His Father (Matthew 27:46-51).

In His prayer in John chapter 17, Jesus utters such meaningful requests, with such adoration of the Father, acknowledging His own position as a man and that of the Father as Giver of all authority (verse 2), as Holy Father (verse 25). This prayer is no last night's performance; it is rather the continuation of a life of previous prayer, as indicated by the phrase **"Father, the hour has now come"** (verse 1).

Jesus's prayer is for:

1. Eternal life for all those the Father has given to Him. Jesus is like the high priest in the Tabernacle, bearing the names of the disciples (and those who will believe through their word, verse 20) on His heart (the Breastplate).
2. The Father to keep the disciples, guarding them all in the Father's own holy name, in unbroken oneness, as the Father and the Son are one (verses 6-12).
3. The Father to sanctify them in His Word of truth, setting the disciples apart to the Father as Jesus Himself had been set apart for the Father; for their impact in the world for the One in them—the Father and the Son (verses 13-21).
4. Glorify the Son (verse 1) to the believers, that they may be perfected in oneness, so that the world may see the love of the Father for His only begotten Son and also the Father's love for His many children (verses 22-26).

This is the prayer for eternal life: **"that they may know You, the only true God, and Jesus Christ whom you have sent"** (John 17:3). Jesus said, **"I am come that they may have life and have it abundantly"** (John 10:10). Eternal life is simply to know the Father and the Son and their oneness, truly, for eternity. This is Jesus's prayer for eternal life; may it also be ours.

Such a fragrance of incense exudes from this deep prayer by the great High Priest for all those in the House of God! Let us also come to the Golden Incense Altars and hence boldly through the Veil to the throne of grace (the Ark of the Covenant), that we may find the mercy and obtain the grace He has prayed for us in this great time of need! (Hebrews 3:6; 4:14-16).

JOSHUA ALTAR
(Joshua 6:1-17)

Whatever God has entrusted into your hands, it is imperative that you execute it faithfully. Joshua had been a warrior since the days of Moses, as evidenced by his role in the battle against the Amalekites (Exodus 17:8-16). At the fall of the wall of Jericho, he opened a new dimension for the conquest of its king and people. Joshua and his nation circled the city in worship—likely in their hearts—and history recorded their smooth victory over Jericho. Beloved, when we come to God in genuine worship, His hand is mobilized to fight our enemies. The destruction of our foes becomes an act of worship to the Lord.

> *"We will obey you just as we obeyed Moses, and may the LORD your God be with you as he was with Moses"* (Joshua 1:17, NLT).

In Joshua chapter eight, the LORD directed Joshua to ascend to Ai and deliver the same defeat that had been inflicted upon Jericho. Afterward, Joshua built an altar and renewed the covenant.

"Then Joshua built an altar unto the LORD God of Israel on Mount Ebal, as Moses, the servant of the LORD, had commanded the children of Israel. As recorded in the book of the law of Moses, the altar was constructed from whole, unhewn stones, over which no man had lifted any iron. On it, they offered burnt offerings and sacrificed peace offerings. Joshua then inscribed on the stones a copy of the law of Moses, written in the presence of the children of Israel. All Israel—with their elders, officers, and judges—stood on one side of the ark and, on the opposite side, before the priests, the Levites who carried the ark of the covenant of the LORD. Both the stranger and the native, half facing Mount Gerizim and half facing Mount Ebal, obeyed Moses' command to bless the people of Israel. After this, Joshua read aloud all the words of the law, including both the blessings and the curses, exactly as written in the book of the law. Not a single word of Moses' command was omitted, as Joshua read before the entire congregation of Israel, including women, children, and resident foreigners" (Joshua 8:30-35).

With Moses, worship was delivered through the law; but with David, it became an expression of relationship. The law compelled the people to gather with the LORD at the altar, even if they did not fully grasp its purpose, they persisted. In contrast, David was drawn to the altar for worship through his personal relationship with the LORD.

Thus, the legacy of the Joshua altar endures as a reminder that worship is not merely ritual but an active, dynamic relationship with

God. As Joshua led his people in obedience, their acts of worship became a catalyst for divine intervention and victory over their foes. May we, too, embrace this spirit of worship, letting our hearts align with God's purpose, so that every step we take is guided by His presence and power.

THE PLACE OF MERCY

The Passover ushered in the total liberation of God's people from bondage, setting them free to become the warriors of worship they were destined to be. This deliverance was accompanied by God's judgment upon the altars of the Egyptians, demonstrating His supreme power over their false gods. In His mercy, God elevated Israel to a higher spiritual walk within His covenant by instituting a continuous priesthood. Sacrifices were offered every morning and evening, and the fire on the altar was never allowed to be extinguished.

> *"And the fire upon the altar shall be burning in it; it shall not be put out: and the priest shall burn wood on it every morning, and lay the burnt offering in order upon it; and he shall burn thereon the fat of the peace offerings. A fire shall ever be burning upon the altar; it shall never go out"* (Leviticus 6:12-13).

Furthermore, the LORD commanded,

> *"And thou shalt command the children of Israel, that they bring thee pure oil beaten for the light, to cause the lamp to burn always. In the tabernacle of the congregation without the*

vail, which is before the testimony, Aaron and his sons shall order it from evening until morning before the LORD: it shall be a statute forever unto their generations on the behalf of the children of Israel" (Exodus 27:20-21).

Before this time, altars were maintained only when required (as seen in Genesis 22 and Genesis 46). However, a perpetual fire upon the altar of sacrifice was instituted, and a select group was set apart for this sacred service. Initially, the firstborn of each family was dedicated to this duty (Exodus 13:12), but later, the Levites were chosen. The LORD spoke to Moses, saying,

"Bring the tribe of Levi near, and present them before Aaron the priest, that they may serve him. And they shall attend to his needs and the needs of the whole congregation before the tabernacle of the meeting, to do the work of the tabernacle. Also they shall attend to all the furnishings of the tabernacle of meeting, and to the needs of the children of Israel, to do the work of the tabernacle. And you shall give the Levites to Aaron and his sons; they are given entirely to him from among the children of Israel. So you shall appoint Aaron and his sons, and they shall attend to their priesthood; but the outsider who comes near shall be put to death." Then the LORD spoke to Moses, saying, "Now behold, I Myself have taken the Levites from among the children of Israel instead of every firstborn who opens the womb among the children of Israel. Therefore the Levites shall be mine" (Numbers 3:5-12).

The sanctity God attached to the altar and its sacrifice led Him to set apart the tribe of Levi so they might minister to the priest, who in turn ministered to the LORD. Strangers—those who had not undergone circumcision and come to salvation—were not allowed to participate in this sacred worship.

The remembrance of our covenant relationship with the LORD should not be confined solely to times of need or divine revelation; rather, it must be a continuous offering in every sphere of our lives—at home, at work, and wherever we have the privilege to serve Him. Moses was instrumental in establishing a pattern of daily worship and sacrifice for the children of Israel, providing not only an ordinance for worship but also a guiding law for their lives.

The first covenant between God and Israel contained detailed regulations for worship and a designated place of worship on earth. The Tabernacle, as designed, had two rooms. The first room—the Holy Place—contained a lampstand, a table, and sacred loaves of bread. Beyond a curtain lay the second room, known as the Most Holy Place, which housed a golden incense altar and the Ark of the Covenant, a wooden chest overlaid with gold on all sides. Within the Ark were kept a golden jar of manna, Aaron's staff that had budded, and the stone tablets of the covenant. Above the Ark were the cherubim of divine glory, whose wings stretched over the cover—the place of atonement. While we cannot detail every aspect of these sacred items now, it is important to understand that once everything was in place, the priests regularly entered the Holy Place to perform their duties, though only the high priest entered the Most Holy Place—and only once a year—to offer blood for his own sins and for the sins of the people who sinned in ignorance (Hebrews 9:1-7, NLT).

The mosaic level of worship initiated a movement toward the sanctity that the body of God's children should embody. Order was established, and a day was set aside for divine worship to the Most High, who had redeemed their lives. No longer were they merely a wandering, downtrodden people; they were a people set apart.

With the inauguration of the covenant and the daily maintenance of worship and sacrifice, God's presence became increasingly manifest among His people. He spoke through Moses, through the mountains, and through the clouds. His presence grew visibly stronger, and His ordinances were observed with greater reverence, for any attempt to break these commandments was met with the consuming fire of His judgment. God is a consuming fire, and His wrath is swift— manifesting in death, pestilence, and other dreadful calamities.

Moses, who instituted a genuine, law-based worship experience, left the people with these final instructions as his departure approached:

> *"These are the statutes and judgments, which you shall be careful to observe in the land which the LORD God of your fathers is giving you to possess, all the days that you live on the earth. You shall utterly destroy all the places where the nations which you shall dispossess served their gods, on the high mountains and on the hills and under every green tree. And you shall destroy their altars, break their sacred pillars, and burn their wooden images with fire; you shall cut down the carved images of their gods and destroy their names from*

that place. You shall not worship the LORD your God with such things. But you shall seek the place where the LORD your God chooses, out of all your tribes, to put His name for His dwelling place; and there you shall go. There you shall take your burnt offerings, your sacrifices, your tithes, the heave offerings of your hand, your vowed offerings, your freewill offerings, and the firstborn of your herds and flocks" (Deuteronomy 12:1-6).

Moses commanded that the Israelites demolish all the altars of the gods of the lands they were about to inherit, so that the memory of those false deities would be completely eradicated from Israel. God understood that if the Israelites allowed these monuments to remain, they would be tempted to fall back into the idolatry of their captors.

We do not own our lives, and just because a particular style of worship in a given center may appeal to our emotions does not make it right. It might satisfy our senses momentarily, but any form of worship that strays from the true throne of God will incur His wrath rather than His blessing—just as when Nadab and Abihu, the sons of Aaron, offered "strange fire" before the LORD.

"And Nadab and Abihu, the sons of Aaron, took either of them his censer, and put fire therein, and put incense thereon, and offered strange fire before the LORD, which He commanded them not. And there went out fire from the LORD, and devoured them, and they died before the LORD" (Leviticus 10:1-2).

The attachments we hold from our former lives—if not cast aside—will ultimately lead to our downfall. We must confess our sins before the LORD, repent, and seek His forgiveness. "There is therefore now no condemnation to them which are in Christ Jesus, who walk not after the flesh, but after the Spirit" (Romans 8:1).

Having released these burdens, what is our next step? "Walk in the Spirit and you shall not fulfill the lust of the flesh" (Galatians 5:16).

We can worship God only in truth and in spirit through our Lord and Savior, Jesus Christ, who directs our worship. The truth is, as we choose to worship God alone, we must relinquish all other powers. In response, God will move to perform miraculous works in and around our lives—works beyond our comprehension.

THE PASSOVER of mercy and favor, as manifested in the life of David, was critical to Israel's survival and divine destiny. David built altars in worship that emitted a sweet-smelling savor to the throne of grace, obtaining mercy for his people. We, too, must practice heartfelt worship if we are to receive God's mercy and favor.

The Bible records only one altar built by David. He desired to purchase Ornan's threshing floor to construct an altar, with the intention of appeasing the mercy of God on behalf of himself and Israel. Although circumstances necessitated this act, we must remember that this occurred during another fourteenth generation. David may not have known that every fourteenth generation of his lineage would reenact this covenant in the times to come, yet he fulfilled his part so that it might not fail in his day.

In David's time, he intended to raise an altar of mercy to avert the wrath of God that had been kindled against him and his people due to his decision to number Israel. In II Samuel 24:1, it is recorded that the LORD was angry with Israel. Consequently, God allowed an attack from Satan as detailed in I Chronicles 21:1-17:

> *And Satan stood up against Israel and provoked David to number Israel. And David said to Joab and to the rulers of the people, "Go, number Israel from Beersheba even to Dan; and bring the number of them to me, that I may know it." And Joab answered, "The LORD make His people a hundred times as numerous as they are, but, my lord the king, are they not all my lord's servants? Why then does my lord require this thing? Why will he cause Israel to sin?" Nevertheless, the king's word prevailed against Joab. Therefore, Joab departed and went throughout all Israel, and came to Jerusalem, and Joab gave the number of the people unto David. And all the people of Israel numbered a thousand thousand and an hundred thousand men that drew the sword; and Judah was four hundred threescore and ten thousand men that drew the sword. But Levi and Benjamin he did not number among them, for the king's word was abominable to Joab. And God was displeased with this; therefore He smote Israel. And David said unto God, "I have sinned greatly because I have done this thing; but now, I beseech You, do away the iniquity of Your servant, for I have done very foolishly." And the LORD spoke unto Gad, David's seer, saying, "Go and tell David,*

saying, 'Thus says the LORD: Choose one of these three things for me to do to you.'" So Gad came to David and said unto him, "Thus says the LORD: 'Choose either three years of famine; or three months of being swept away before your enemies, while the sword of your enemies pursues you; or three days of the sword of the LORD, even the pestilence, in the land, with the angel of the LORD destroying throughout all the coasts of Israel.' Now therefore advise yourself what word I shall bring again to him who sent me." And David said unto Gad, "I am in great strait; let me fall into the hand of the LORD, for His mercies are very great; but do not let me fall into the hand of man." So the LORD sent pestilence upon Israel, and there fell of Israel seventy thousand men. And God sent an angel unto Jerusalem to destroy it; and as he was destroying, the LORD saw, and He repented of the evil, and said to the angel, "It is enough; now restrain your hand." And the angel of the LORD stood by the threshing floor of Ornan the Jebusite. And David lifted up his eyes and saw the angel of the LORD standing between the earth and the heaven, with a drawn sword in his hand stretched over Jerusalem. Then David and the elders of Israel, who were clothed in sackcloth, fell upon their faces. And David said unto God, "Is it not I that commanded the people to be numbered? Even I have sinned and done evil indeed; but as for these sheep, what have they done? Let Your hand, I pray Thee, O LORD my God, be upon me and on my father's house, but not upon Your people, that they should be plagued."

The mercy of God is essential for all, especially for those in the household of faith, so that we do not provoke His wrath. The scriptures remind us, "It is a terrible thing to fall into the hands of the living God" (Hebrews 10:31, NLT). David was establishing this very thing.

> *Then the angel of the LORD commanded Gad to tell David to go up and set up an altar unto the LORD in the threshing floor of Ornan the Jebusite. David obeyed Gad's message, spoken in the name of the LORD. Ornan, upon seeing the angel with his four sons hiding, left the threshing floor where he was threshing wheat. When David arrived, Ornan bowed to him with his face to the ground. David then said, "Grant me the place of this threshing floor, that I may build an altar there unto the LORD. Grant it to me for the full price, so that the plague may be stayed from the people." And Ornan said, "Take it, and let my lord the king do that which is good in his eyes; behold, I give you the oxen also for burnt offerings, and the threshing instruments for wood, and the wheat for the meat offering. I give it all." But King David replied, "No; I will certainly purchase it for the full price, for I will not take that which is yours for the LORD, nor offer burnt offerings without cost." So David paid Ornan six hundred shekels of gold by weight. Then David built an altar unto the LORD, offered burnt offerings and peace offerings, and called on the LORD; and the LORD answered him from heaven with fire upon the*

altar of burnt offering. The LORD then commanded the angel, and he withdrew his sword back into its sheath. When David saw that the LORD had answered him at the threshing floor of Ornan the Jebusite, he sacrificed there (I Chronicles 21:18-28).

This mercy and favor manifested in David's life led Solomon to testify in prayer, "You have shown great mercy to David my father, and have made me king in his place" (II Chronicles 1:8, NKJV).

Beloved, we need the great mercy of God to stand firm continually. God alone bestows mercy. Whether you are a cell leader, pastor, or servant leader of God, you must rely on His mercy to avoid incurring His wrath upon those you lead. Even as a father in the home, only God's mercy can keep evil at bay. This was the divine mandate for Israel as another fourteenth generation passed.

As a result of David's communion with the LORD while tending his sheep and leading them to pasture, he had established an altar relationship with the LORD and was empowered by the Spirit of God. No wonder he was unafraid when facing Goliath; he confronted him and secured victory. This is not far-fetched. David consistently took time to worship at his altar—often playing his harp, perhaps seated on a rock in solitude with his sheep—bringing heaven's glory down to earth.

Through David's example, we learned that worship alone could cast out devils. In his day, whenever David played the harp, Saul was delivered from the torment of the evil spirits that plagued him. Some strongholds troubling our lineage may not respond to the command, "I cast you out in Jesus' name," but they yield when the wind of the Holy Spirit blows through their domain, clearing territories we once thought unconquerable. This wind of the Spirit flows easily through genuine worship, granting us territories and blessings beyond our imagination.

Just as Noah raised the first altar, David's altars in worship produced a sweet-smelling savor before the throne of grace and secured mercy for his people. We must embrace a lifestyle of worship, beloved, if we desire to receive God's mercy and favor.

Questions for Reflection

1. Abraham and his descendants sought the Lord for direction through their worship of Him. In what ways do you seek the Lord's direction in your life?

2. Moses established a continuous worship experience for the children of Israel. How and where do you worship God?

3. The Israelites were to destroy all of evidence of false worship and idolatry before dwelling in the promised land so that they would not be tempted to forsake God. Is there something in your life that takes the place of God? What can you do to remove it from your life?

4. David invoked the wrath of God for both his people and himself, so he called on the mercy of God. When have you called on God for His mercy for either yourself or someone else? What were the results? Write a prayer of thanks to God for what He did.

5. David's relationship with God gave him the confidence to face Goliath and the courage to play his harp in the presence of the evil spirit within Saul. How has your relationship with God enabled you to have confidence or courage?

CHAPTER 5

JOSIAH'S ALTARS

"There had been no Passover kept in Israel like that since the days of Samuel the prophet; and none of the kings of Israel had kept such a Passover as Josiah kept, with the priests, the Levites, all Judah and Israel who were present, and the inhabitants of Jerusalem" (II Chronicles 35:18).

God visited His people again around another fourteenth generation from David, and the greatest celebration at the altar occurred under Josiah's leadership (II Chronicles 35:16). David had worshiped at this sacred place, but Solomon established it as a temple. From the days of Abraham, the Lord ordained that He would visit His people every fourteenth generation, with each visit reminding them of His covenant from different perspectives.

Solomon built the temple at this location (II Chronicles 3:1), and Josiah chose it to magnify God's glory, acknowledging His covenantal protection over their lives. Just as God's covenant brings blessings, the enemy can use ancestral covenants to afflict those whose forefathers served idols. These bonds often linger for three or four generations (Exodus 20:5), but every act of renewal strengthens

God's covenant. After fourteen generations, however, the potency of the covenant can wane.

The Feast of Unleavened Bread, a seven-day celebration that began the day after Passover, commemorated Israel's exodus from Egypt (Exodus 12:14-20). For seven days, they ate bread without yeast, just as their ancestors did, symbolizing haste in preparation for deliverance. This feast reminded the people of their journey from bondage to freedom.

Many Christians today forget the liberty they have in Christ (John 8:32), entangling themselves in minor issues. They tremble before the devil, forgetting that Christ's victory has placed them far above all principalities and powers (Ephesians 2:1-7). Consider this: if we have authority over the devil, what threat does he pose? None. Can an ant bar a homeowner from entering his house? Certainly not. Therefore, the enemy has no right to rule over us. Jesus has freed and empowered us: "Greater is He who is in you than he who is in the world" (I John 4:4).

Continuous communion at the altar ensures a continual renewal of God's power in our lives. As we spend time expressing love through worship and praise, our awareness of His presence grows. This communion strengthens our faith, reminding us of the Holy Spirit's power and authority over Satan.

When Moses ascended Mount Sinai and remained for forty days and nights, his face shone with God's glory upon his return, causing fear among the Israelites (Exodus 34:30). Beloved, the enemy fears us when we radiate God's presence. Let us never neglect our time with the Most Holy God.

JOSIAH TOOK STEPS TO FREEDOM

"For in the eighth year of his reign, while he was still young, he began to seek the God of his father David; and in the twelfth year, he began to purge Judah and Jerusalem of high places, Asherah poles, carved images, and cast idols" (II Chronicles 34:3).

True freedom requires purging all that offends God to be blameless before Him. Josiah eradicated idolatry from Judah, striving to please and honor the one true God (Exodus 20:3-4). To enter genuine freedom, we must remove every form of idolatry from our lives—anything that rivals God's authority.

Some may claim, "I bow to no one but God; idolatry isn't my problem." Yet, the Holy Spirit can reveal hidden altars we unknowingly serve. Paul warned the Corinthians: "Do you not know that the unrighteous will not inherit the kingdom of God? Do not be deceived: Neither fornicators, nor idolaters, nor adulterers, nor effeminate, nor sodomites, nor thieves, nor covetous, nor drunkards, nor revilers, nor extortioners will inherit the kingdom of God" (I Corinthians 6:9-10).

God calls us to freedom in Christ, not bondage in sin. Cry out to Him today: "In everything you were enriched in Him—in all speech and knowledge—just as the testimony about Christ was confirmed in you.

You do not lack any spiritual gift as you eagerly wait for our Lord Jesus Christ to be revealed. He will also strengthen you to the end, so that you will be blameless on the day of our Lord Jesus Christ. God is faithful; you were called by Him into fellowship with His Son, Jesus Christ our Lord" (I Corinthians 1:5-9).

In 2 Chronicles 34:3-5, Josiah took step to remove structured altars that were raised against the God of Israel. If I was in Josiah's mind, the question would be how did we get here fourteen generations down the line from David the great king? All the forces of earth and nature were consecrated to the lord but are now being used to sacrifice to some demon god of fertility. The irony of this situation is not far fetched from believers today who leave the one who is the source of all things and start worshipping things. We were not wired to live our lives begging for things. We were programmed to be fruitful from the beginning and all the things about our lives have already been supplied before we came but like Jeremiah said when we leave the one who is the fountain of life and we start building cisterns.

Josiah knew God could not inhabit His temple while idolatry thrived. He demolished Asherah poles, carved images, and idols that had replaced God's sanctified objects. Remarkably, Hilkiah found the long-neglected Book of the Law written by Moses. That the book was "found" implies it had been forgotten. In the beginning, it was meant to be read day and night, but dust had settled on it through years of neglect.

My father often said it is better to grow up in a godly family and accept Christ without first being lost in the world. Although God can redeem the worst situations, scars and consequences often linger. Even after redemption, past choices can haunt us.

Josiah was one of the greatest reformers in biblical history. He dismantled everything that had replaced the national altar and called the people back to God, much like Elijah did. During Josiah's reign, Judah kept God's ordinances, and the altar fire never went out.

We each have opportunities to serve God. Josiah's zeal brought Judah back to God, and he influenced his generation to honor the Lord. How are you wielding your influence today? Commit yourself to leading those around you back to God, just as Josiah did.

Questions for Reflection

1. Communion with God is an encounter with not only His immense power in our lives but also over Satan. Ephesians 6:10 instructs us, "...be strong in the Lord and in the power of His might." Then, verses 11-18 tell us to put on the whole armor of God so that we can stand against the devil. List what God wants you to do to prepare for spiritual battle:

   a)

   b)

   c)

   d)

   e)

2. King Josiah intentionally purged evil from the land and the people under his reign. Take inventory of your surroundings and your activities. Are there some belongings, some activities, or some habits that are taking the place of God or interfering with your relationship with Him and your worship of Him? What can you do today to purge them from your life?

CHAPTER 6

OTHER SIGNIFICANT ALTARS

JACOB: ALTARS FOR DIRECTION

There is a saying that the world will make way for the one who knows where he is going. In Jacob's case, he needed direction—and he received it. When our hearts are knit to God and all we desire is to think of and do His will, a time comes when our thoughts perfectly align with His.

The moment Jacob learned that Joseph was still alive, he declared, "It is enough; Joseph my son is yet alive: I will go and see him before I die" (Genesis 45:28). Although he had not formally sought God's counsel at that moment, his will was already merged with God's, so he instinctively knew the right course of action. This natural alignment is the fruit of genuine communion with the Divine. Others might have sent Joseph's brothers back to him, insisting that he see his father first before his father came to him. While that approach is not entirely wrong, truly understanding the mind of the Spirit requires an unwavering commitment to Him. Recall Genesis 28, when Jacob witnessed angels ascending and descending on a ladder that reached into heaven; even then, he knew that his journey was far from complete. This divine encounter was a milestone, yet it also served as a reminder that the pursuit of God's guidance is an ongoing process—one that continually refines and directs his path.

Although Jacob appeared to have a partial understanding of God's will, he never took a decisive step without first consulting with Him at the altar of communion. Genesis 46 recounts that on his journey to Egypt, Jacob paused at Beersheba to offer sacrifices to God. That night, God spoke to him, confirming His will for Jacob to go down to Egypt. Hebrews 11:6 affirms that God rewards those who diligently seek Him. In response to Jacob's earnest prayer, God led him to Egypt to bless and enlarge his family. For many, Egypt symbolized a place of destruction and bondage; yet for Jacob, it became the setting where his family would be enlarged and the nation of Israel would be born, just as God had promised. Jacob's experience demonstrates that true direction from God comes through consistent communion at the altar, where divine confirmation guides our steps even into seemingly ominous places.

Have you been discerning where the Lord is calling you to go? Sometimes, well-meaning friends or advisors offer guidance that conflicts with God's plan, steering you toward a wilderness of confusion and unnecessary tribulation. When you follow their counsel instead of God's, you risk wandering down a path that leads away from His blessings. God, however, knows the future intricately—even the obstacles hidden along misguided paths. Following His plan opens up a future filled with hope, as Jeremiah 29:11 assures us: "For I know the plans I have for you," declares the LORD, "plans to prosper you and not to harm you, plans to give you hope and a future." When you align your direction with God's will, every step brings glory to Him and secures your destiny. The journey may be difficult, but His guidance transforms every hardship into a stepping stone toward His divine promise.

God's direction in a person's life is invaluable. This is why Moses pleaded with God that if He would not accompany them, they should not leave their current place (Exodus 33:14-15). We need clear guidance to ensure we do not miss the abundant blessings that God has prepared. Even when you follow a path you believe is led by the Lord, encountering difficulties does not mean He is absent. As Matthew 7:14 reminds us, "...narrow is the gate and difficult is the way which leads to life, and there are few who find it." When challenges arise, it is essential to seek God's wisdom and remain steadfast in His direction. Embracing His guidance means trusting that every trial is part of His larger plan for you. His direction provides the clarity needed to navigate life's uncertainties and to continue moving forward with confidence in His promises. With His light illuminating your path, you are less likely to be sidetracked by worldly distractions or false counsel, ensuring that your spiritual journey remains true to His calling.

THE MAN OF GOD: ALTARS CONTROLLING OTHER FORCES

God had chosen Jerusalem as the place where He would be worshipped, but when the kingdom split after Solomon's death,

Jeroboam seized control of ten tribes. In his haste to consolidate power, Jeroboam quickly instituted a priesthood that was not recognized by Yahweh, thereby diverting the hearts of the people away from God. His actions were driven by the fear that if Jerusalem remained the sole acceptable place of worship for Yahweh, the people would continue to flock there—threatening the new kingdom he had just acquired. In his effort to secure his throne, Jeroboam established alternative altars, intentionally diverting worship away from the true temple in Jerusalem.

The devil soon took control of these newly raised altars because, if they were not consecrated to the Lord, they were, by default, dedicated to the devil. It is evident that the enemy quickly assigned his principal agents to seize control over these altars, and the truth emerged that demons had dominion over much of the land of Israel. I Kings 13 recounts that while Jeroboam was at one of these strange altars, preparing to burn incense, a man of God came by the word of the Lord to deliver a message. Notably, when the young man appeared at the altar, his declaration was both authoritative and forceful—a clear sign that divine power was still at work, even amid widespread apostasy.

Then the man of God cried out against the altar by the word of the Lord, saying, "O altar, altar! Thus says the Lord: 'Behold, a child, Josiah by name, shall be born to the house of David; and on you he shall sacrifice the priests of the high places who burn incense on you, and men's bones shall be burned on you.' And he gave a sign that same day, saying, 'This is the sign which the Lord has spoken: Surely the altar shall split apart, and the ashes on it shall be poured out.' So it came to pass when King Jeroboam heard the word of the man of God, who cried out against the altar in Bethel, that he stretched out his hand from the altar, saying, 'Arrest him!' Then his hand, which he stretched out toward the man of God, withered, so that he could not pull it back to himself. The altar also split apart, and the ashes poured out, exactly as the man of God had declared by the word of the Lord" (I Kings 13:2-5, NKJV). This dramatic event was a powerful testament to the reality that when altars are not raised to the Lord, they become instruments of the enemy.

No man receives the anointing of the Holy Spirit until he has established an altar of communion with God. Today, I see many who attempt to turn the anointing into a form of magic, believing that a three-day dry fast will automatically bestow on them the fullness of the Spirit. However, God releases His anointing only on those who are truly ready to be in His presence. When desperate individuals fail to receive the anointing they so ardently desire, they often resort to diabolical measures, seeking power at any cost. Yet, God is never in a hurry; He has a specific process charted out for each one of us to empower us for His service. God alone can anoint us to do His will, and we cannot skip any steps because He is not a respecter of persons. Our spiritual growth must occur in proper order, with each step preparing us for the next, ensuring that we are thoroughly equipped to carry out His purposes.

The man of God in I Kings 13 had faithfully walked with the Lord, which is why God chose him to carry out the task of tearing down the altars and pulling down the demonic forces ruling in Israel—even though he was from Judah. This should challenge us to reflect: before being sent to destroy the forces that oppress a nation, a man of God must have an established altar of communion with the Lord in his own community. Without that intimate, personal foundation, our efforts to break strongholds can fall short. It is through sustained communion that the Spirit empowers us to confront and overcome the powers of darkness. Our connection to God is the channel through which His anointing flows, equipping us to engage in spiritual warfare effectively and to dismantle every stronghold that the enemy sets up.

We are empowered to transform lives shackled by the enemy only when our relationship with the Lord deepens. Jesus called the twelve disciples to be with Him so that He could send them out to preach and cast out devils, effectively dismantling the controlling forces of darkness (Mark 3:13-14). However, before they embarked on that mission, they spent time in His presence, learning from Him, so that their lives would not mimic the patterns of the world. True spiritual authority is not inherited from worldly power but is acquired through intimate communion with God. When we align our lives with His purpose, we gain not only direction and anointing for controlling external forces but also the capacity to steer our own destiny in harmony with His will. God provides us with clear instructions on how to enter into, and exit from, the altar—guidelines that protect us from spiritual contamination and harm. This pathway, marked by the ways of the Spirit, is essential for walking victoriously in a world filled with opposition.

Beloved, there are divinely orchestrated ways to engage the enemy in battle, and if we do not adhere to these spiritual paths, we risk falling into disarray. While Jesus walked this earth, He always knew the safest routes to take—even when His life was in imminent danger from those who sought to kill Him. As recorded in John 7:1 (NKJV), "After these things Jesus walked in Galilee: for He did not want to walk in Judea, because the Jews sought to kill Him." Jesus demonstrated that divine guidance is crucial in avoiding spiritual pitfalls and ensuring safety. The Holy Spirit reveals the right path, and when we remain sensitive to His voice, we can navigate even the most treacherous spiritual landscapes. This is the same divine wisdom that must guide us today, as we seek to dismantle every demonic stronghold that attempts to intrude upon our spiritual lives.

David, one of the great men of God, would not go into battle until he had heard from the Lord. He was meticulous about seeking divine instruction regarding when and how to confront his enemies, regardless of his previous successes. This dependency on God's word ensured that his strategies were divinely inspired and effective. Likewise, Elijah, in his fierce confrontation with the prophets of Baal, boldly declared, "Let it be known this day that You are God in Israel and I am Your servant, and that I have done all these things at Your word" (1 Kings 18:36, NKJV). Such examples illustrate that the foundation of any victorious battle is built upon the consistent pursuit of God's guidance. We must therefore equip ourselves by immersing in His Word, praying for discernment, and aligning our every step with His divine plan. When we do so, we secure not only our personal victories but also contribute to the advancement of God's kingdom, ensuring that His glory is manifested through our lives.

At the altar, you not only receive direction and anointing for controlling external forces, but you also gain the ability to shape your own destiny in alignment with God's purpose. When God instructed the man of God, He provided explicit guidance on how to approach the altar, and also on how to depart from it safely. These instructions were not arbitrary; they were the ways of the Spirit, carefully designed to enable him to tread without injury or contamination. It is essential that we, too, learn these spiritual pathways—how to enter into the presence of God, how to receive His anointing, and how to exit with our spirit unblemished. Such knowledge is vital because, in our daily lives, we face battles that extend beyond the physical realm. Without adhering to the divine protocols, we risk being ensnared by the enemy's schemes, which can lead to spiritual compromise and defeat. Embracing God's methods ensures that every step we take is shielded by His power and grace, leading us to fulfill our destiny as conquerors in Christ.

The enemy delights in exploiting every opportunity to sever our connection with the Spirit of God and to keep us from experiencing unity within the body of Christ. When we allow internal discord, pride, or misguided ambitions to take root, we inadvertently build altars of affliction that hinder our spiritual growth and weaken the Church. Such altars act as barriers, preventing the free flow of God's blessings and His unifying love. They not only fracture our personal relationships but also create a spiritual vacuum in which the enemy can operate unchecked. It is, therefore, imperative that we actively dismantle these altars of affliction. By rejecting divisive behaviors and embracing a spirit of unity and love, we can ensure that our homes, hearts, and communities remain fortified against the forces of darkness. In doing so, we not only protect ourselves but also contribute to a stronger, more unified Church that reflects the true character of Christ. As we stand together in faith, we build a resilient spiritual foundation that resists all attempts by the enemy to sow discord, ensuring that God's light continues to shine brightly in every aspect of our lives.

HEZEKIAH: ALTARS THAT BRING REVIVAL

No genuine revival can occur without first raising an altar dedicated to that purpose. Martin Luther recognized the urgent need for reformation and, in response, raised an altar to the Lord in his day. I believe the inspiration to write his ninety-five theses was sparked at that very altar, and those theses ultimately ignited the fire of reformation. Such altars are not mere structures; they are the sacred settings from which revival is born, drawing the hearts of believers back to God in a time of spiritual drought.

Hezekiah was born into a legacy of wickedness—his father was one of the most corrupt and ruthless kings Judah had ever produced. In stark contrast, Hezekiah's heart was resolutely fixed on doing the will of God. Despite the oppressive environment of his family, where even the act of worship might have incurred the lethal wrath of his father, Hezekiah persisted. He secretly established a personal altar of communion with the Lord, crying out for the revival of Judah with a passion that defied his perilous circumstances. This act of covert devotion required immense courage and spiritual maturity. Even while serving as co-regent with his tyrannical father, Hezekiah spoke with wisdom and conviction, urging a return to godly principles. His commitment was so profound that elements of Solomon's wisdom found their way into the teachings of his contemporaries, as recorded in Proverbs 25:1. Hezekiah's legacy reminds us that true revival begins with a heart dedicated to God, even in the midst of overwhelming adversity.

The prayer of Hezekiah on his secret altar was answered in a remarkable and transformative way when his wicked father died. Although Hezekiah may not have explicitly prayed for his father's demise, his heartfelt cry for revival was met with divine intervention. In the very first month of his reign, Hezekiah initiated the revival he had long yearned for. With divine boldness, he reopened the temple that his father had closed, summoning all the priests to resume their sacred duty of leading worship. Hezekiah also instructed the people to provide for the temple's needs according to the law, ensuring that every aspect of worship was restored. As a result, joy was restored to the nation; untold hardships subsided, and even the prolonged wars came to an end. The priests were rejuvenated, and the needs of the impoverished were met. In the second month of his reign, Hezekiah expanded the revival by calling together not only all of Judah but also the remnant of Israel, uniting the people in a renewed commitment to God's covenant. This comprehensive revival was a direct response to

Hezekiah's earnest prayers at his secret altar—a testament to the power of intimate communion with God.

For us to be the revival of the Church that will usher in the coming of the Lord Jesus Christ, we must begin by calling upon the Lord with all our heart. When we diligently seek Him, He infuses our lives with joy and renewed purpose. The historical example of revival, such as the collapse of communism in Russia influenced by impassioned cries from devout believers, stands as a powerful reminder of what God can accomplish when His people unite in prayer. Today, our world desperately needs a return to God. Revival of souls on a global scale is imperative, for no enemy can withstand the fire of true revival. We must rise from spiritual slumber and earnestly ask God to open the gates of divine visitation in our lives, our families, and our communities. By embracing consistent prayer and worship, we not only secure our own spiritual freedom but also become catalysts for transformation in a world starved for God's light. In doing so, we lay the foundation for a future where God's glory is unmistakably evident.

Questions for Reflection

1. Jacob consulted God for direction. When was the last time you asked God to direct you in a decision, a plan, or an opportunity? In what ways did He guide you?

2. The man of God knew the specific directions God had given him, but he allowed an old prophet to deceive him. Because he listened to a man instead of God, he lost his life. When are you tempted to listen to others instead of God? What steps can you take to guard yourself from this happening?

3. What are you doing daily to stay in tune with God's will and direction for your life?

4. What can you do to spark revival in your family? In your church? In your community?

CHAPTER 7

TODAY'S ALTARS

The context in which the word "altar" is frequently used in the Christian circle today often refers to the family altar—a time when a Christian household gathers in the morning or evening for devotions. However, it is important to note that altars can also be maintained individually; this personal practice is typically called "quiet time." In both cases, the altar represents a sacred space set aside for communion with the Lord. It is at this place that we intentionally draw near to God, seeking His guidance and presence above all else. The altar is not merely a physical location or routine; it is a spiritual posture that reflects our commitment to prioritize our relationship with Him. In our hectic world, maintaining such sacred time is both a challenge and a necessity. The true essence of the altar remains in our willingness to set aside distractions and create intentional space for divine encounter, a practice that has been central to the faith of generations past and remains vital today.

The fast-paced nature of today's society greatly affects the way Christians approach their altars. In our modern world, schedules are overwhelmingly packed, leaving little room for the patience required to create uninterrupted time for deep communion with our Lord in the quietness of solitude. Many believers attempt to fit in prayer or Bible reading during moments of transit—on a noisy bus or while commuting—where distractions abound and true intimacy with God becomes nearly impossible. In such environments, the essence of intimate communion is compromised; the noise and constant movement can drown out the still small voice of God. One may wonder whether anyone can genuinely experience the fullness of God's presence when their surroundings are anything but peaceful. This is not intended as judgment but as a thought-provoking reminder that God desires our full, undivided attention at the altar. The examples set forth in Scripture show us that when we approach the altar with intentionality, we create space for divine revelation, deep spiritual insight, and a more profound alignment with God's will.

Meanwhile, in the Old Testament, the practice of maintaining an altar was both sacred and consistent. The priest was required to offer sacrifices on the altar every day, a discipline that underscored the importance of continual devotion. The fire on the altar had to be kept burning without interruption; each morning, the priest would add fresh wood to the flame, arrange the burnt offerings, and then burn the fat of the peace offerings. This ritual was not merely a routine but a vital act of worship—a continual burnt offering that symbolized the everlasting nature of God's covenant with His people. The fire, which must never go out, represented God's eternal presence and the constant outpouring of His grace (Leviticus 6:12-13, NLT). Such a disciplined, daily act of devotion reminds us that true communion with God requires consistency and reverence. In our lives today, replicating this level of commitment may seem challenging, yet it is essential if we are to experience the transformative power of God's presence. It is in this persistent, sacred routine that the heart of worship is truly kindled.

Now, consider the specific instructions given for the offerings upon the altar, as detailed in Exodus 29:38-42. This passage commands that two lambs of the first year be offered daily—one in the morning and the other in the evening. Alongside the lambs, a tenth of a deal of flour mixed with a quarter of a hin of beaten oil and a quarter of a hin of wine for a drink offering is to be presented. The offering is described as a continual burnt offering—a sacrifice made by fire unto the Lord that produces a sweet-smelling aroma, pleasing to Him. This ritual was not a one-time event; it was to be carried out day by day throughout the generations, right at the door of the tabernacle of the congregation, where God would meet His people and speak to them. The detailed instructions emphasize not only the importance of the sacrifice itself but also the necessity of doing it in a prescribed, orderly manner. In our modern context, this serves as a metaphor for the disciplined practice of our spiritual devotions. When we approach our personal altars—whether in quiet solitude or with our families— we too should do so with order, intentionality, and reverence, ensuring that our worship is a continuous, sweet-smelling offering to the Lord.

No sacrifice is made without a deliberate, intentional effort to achieve its inherent result: the releasing of a sweet-smelling aroma to the Lord and the immediate manifestation of His glory through the fellowship experienced at the altar table. The process of communion with God is not something that can be rushed or performed haphazardly. Yet, this is precisely what is happening today in many circles—people are attempting to mimic these sacred practices in environments filled with distractions and noise, thereby diluting the depth and effectiveness of their spiritual communion. The haste with which some try to conduct their devotions results in a watered-down experience that fails to bring the full benefits of intimate fellowship with God. The rich symbolism of the altar—its consistent, daily, and orderly practice—calls us to a higher standard of devotion, one that honors God's design for true worship and enables His glory to fill our lives completely.

TIMING AND SACRIFICE

1. DAILY PERSONAL ALTAR

Today, there are long lists for a person to scan through when searching for an outlined daily devotional for personal or family use. Though devotionals are valuable tools that guide us into communion at the altar with the Lord, they are not meant to be used mechanically without genuine, heartfelt contact with the Holy Spirit. Their purpose, whether through group discussion or personal meditation, is to direct our thoughts toward worship and to help us be still in the presence of our Lord. Quiet time—another term for personal devotion—should be entered into with mindfulness and earnestness, as it is the time set aside to meet with our holy God. Personally, I have experienced deep communion with God through times of worship, moments of silence, scripture reading, and by attending to prayer burdens that He has placed on my heart. This intimate time is essential to keep our spiritual connection strong and to ensure that we remain aligned with God's purpose throughout our daily lives.

Naturally, however you connect with His presence, it is essential to allow for flexibility under the guidance of the Holy Spirit so that He might lead you. It is when the Spirit takes the lead that our devotional time truly becomes a vibrant communion with God. This communion does not simply end when our quiet time concludes; rather, it continues to permeate our entire day. When we invite God to lead our hearts from the very start, His presence carries us through every moment. We begin the day with a spirit of worship that accompanies us wherever we go. In essence, our daily communion acts as a spiritual anchor, ensuring that regardless of the chaos around us, we remain centered in His love and guidance. The scripture reminds us, "The fire shall ever be burning upon the altar; it shall never go out" (Leviticus 6:13). This unceasing fire symbolizes the constant, dynamic energy of God's presence in our lives—a presence that fuels our strength, inspires our decisions, and provides clarity even in the midst of our busiest hours. By yielding to the Holy Spirit's gentle lead during our quiet time, we allow God's transformative power to ripple throughout our day, ensuring that every action and thought is imbued with His divine purpose.

One reason why we long to be with the Lord in communion is that our love for Him is all-consuming. As Professor Zacharias Tanee Fomum wisely noted, "When a person loves someone, he always enjoys talking to the person he loves, regardless of the occasion." This deep affection compels us to seek constant fellowship with the Lord. Our hearts crave the intimate dialogue that only He can provide, and our souls are refreshed in His presence. This longing to commune with God is not merely about fulfilling a duty but about nurturing a relationship that brings us indescribable joy and peace. When we truly love God, we desire to know Him more fully and to reflect His love in every aspect of our lives. That deep, personal connection is the essence of our worship and the very foundation upon which our spiritual lives are built.

A similar illustration of this longing can be found in the nature of intimate relationships between lovers. There are moments and words that true lovers reserve only for each other—conversations too delicate or profound to be shared in public. While there is no inherent need to hide these expressions, the very nature of deep love often calls for private moments of vulnerability and authenticity. The more intense the love between two people, the greater their desire to share personal thoughts and feelings away from the prying eyes of the world. In much the same way, our relationship with God flourishes in the intimacy of personal communion, free from distractions and external influences. This secluded time at our altar of devotion enables us to experience God's love in a profoundly personal way, deepening our understanding of His will. When we set aside dedicated moments for private worship, we create a sacred space where our hearts can truly open to His voice, fostering a relationship that nurtures and sustains us in all aspects of life.

Beloved, if you wish to avoid frustration in your relationship with the

Lord, it is imperative to deliberately set up your personal altar of sacrifice so that it releases a sweet-smelling savor at the proper time— just as in the days of Moses, when the morning and evening sacrifices were observed diligently. In those ancient times, the people labored continuously to maintain the altar, and nothing could disrupt that sacred routine. You are encouraged to do the same. A well-established personal altar is not a one-time event but a continual, deliberate practice of devotion. It is an act of surrender and renewal that reaffirms your commitment to God each day. By setting aside time for intentional worship, prayer, and meditation, you allow His presence to transform your heart and mind. This dedicated time becomes the launching pad for your day, infusing every moment with His guidance and grace. When you consistently return to your personal altar, you fortify your spiritual life, ensuring that no matter what challenges arise, you remain anchored in His love and purpose.

When lovers meet, they explore each other's inner worlds— discovering thoughts, desires, motives, likes, and dislikes. There is an insatiable desire to understand one another on a deeper level and to share personal truths that are reserved for private moments. This longing to know each other more intimately mirrors our desire for deeper communion with God. Just as lovers need moments of withdrawal from the public eye to fully connect and express their true selves, we too must create private moments to commune with the Lord. In these quiet, undisturbed times, we uncover the rich depths of His character, and our understanding of His will grows exponentially. This sacred time of withdrawal from the demands of everyday life is essential for fostering a profound relationship with the Divine. It is in these moments that we receive fresh insights, healing, and strength—allowing us to face the world with renewed passion and clarity. Such intimate communion deepens our love for God, enhances our spiritual sensitivity, and equips us to live out His purpose with conviction.

There is no greater place for fellowship than at the altar. In the beginning, God and Adam met "at the cool of the day" simply to commune with each other. This model of divine fellowship is foundational to our understanding of intimacy with God. The more of God we know, the more of His presence we carry, and the more our lives radiate His fire—whether in our personal testimony or from the pulpit when we preach. It is important to note that the pulpit is not synonymous with the altar. For instance, in days past, men like John Hyde canceled their pulpit appointments to spend time with the Lord, recognizing that nothing could substitute for personal communion. Jesus Himself prioritized spending time with His Father over addressing every need for healing and deliverance among the people. This intentional withdrawal into personal communion underscores the necessity of cultivating a deep, ongoing relationship with God. In our modern world, where distractions abound, the altar remains the ultimate sanctuary—a place where our souls are nourished and our spiritual fire is kindled.

At even, when the sun set, people brought to Jesus all who were diseased or possessed by devils, and the entire city gathered at His feet. He healed many of diverse diseases and cast out numerous devils, not permitting them to speak, for they recognized His authority. In the early morning, rising well before daybreak, Jesus withdrew to a solitary place to pray, and Simon along with those who were with Him followed. When they found Him, they exclaimed, "All men seek for thee" (Mark 1:32-37). This pattern of withdrawing into solitary prayer and then emerging to minister to others reveals the importance of the personal altar. It is at this sacred place of quiet communion that divine strength is replenished, and the healing power of God is unleashed to transform lives. In our own lives, emulating Jesus' discipline of early morning communion is vital. It ensures that we begin each day anchored in His presence, ready to face the challenges ahead and to extend His love and healing to a hurting world.

Jesus considered this time of communion so essential that He set aside the very best time and the most suitable place to be with His heavenly Father. His desire was not for self-display or personal glory, but solely to commune with the One who created and sustains Him. This was not an isolated occurrence; rather, it was a regular practice in His life. How could He reach spiritual fulfillment without consistently setting aside time to be with His Father? How could He afford to be adrift and disconnected from the source of all life? The discipline of daily communion was foundational to His ministry, empowering Him to carry out His divine mission. As believers, we are called to emulate this example—prioritizing intimate moments with our Creator over the distractions of the world. It is in these moments of pure, unmediated encounter with God that our true strength is revealed and our lives are transformed.

John Wesley, the father of Methodism, is a profound example of this principle. Every day, between 4 a.m. and 6 a.m., Wesley set aside time to commune with his Lord. Without this time of intimate fellowship, he would not have recorded the remarkable success of his ministry. There is a marked difference between merely thinking or brainstorming and truly communing with the Lord. Wesley's disciplined routine of early morning devotion allowed him to receive fresh insights, guidance, and strength, which he then poured into his ministry. His life is a testament to the transformative power of daily communion with God—a practice that not only renews the spirit but also ignites a passion for service and a deep commitment to His purpose. Let us, too, set aside regular time to be alone with God, allowing His presence to infuse every aspect of our lives and empower us to fulfill the calling He has placed on our hearts.

> *"And the LORD said unto Moses, "Come up to Me into the mount, and be there: and I will give thee tables of stone, and a law, and commandments which I have written; that thou mayest teach them." Moses then rose with his minister Joshua and went up into the mount of God. He instructed the elders, "Tarry ye here for us until we come again unto you: behold, Aaron and Hur are with you; if any man have any matters to do, let him come unto them." As Moses ascended the mount, a cloud covered it, and the glory of the LORD abided upon Mount Sinai for six days; on the seventh day, God called unto Moses from the midst of the cloud. The sight of the glory of the LORD was like devouring fire atop the mount in the eyes of*

the children of Israel. Moses remained in the cloud for forty days and forty nights (Exodus 24:12-18).

This powerful encounter illustrates the importance of setting aside dedicated, undisturbed time to be in God's presence—a practice that forms the very foundation of our spiritual lives.

As stated in the above scripture, Moses had quiet time with the Lord when he was invited. For six days, he rested in silence before the Almighty, and on the seventh day, God began to speak to him. Perhaps Moses needed those six days to clear his mind of worldly distractions, preparing his heart to fully receive the voice of the Lord. This intentional period of quiet reflection is a critical component of effective communion with God. Without such a sacred pause, our hearts remain cluttered, and the divine message may never penetrate the noise of our busy lives. The discipline Moses practiced is a model for us today—a reminder that deep, transformative communion requires not only time but also a deliberate withdrawal from the clamor of daily existence.

The lyrics of songwriter Don Moen explains this deeply:

"I just want to be where You are, dwelling daily in Your presence. I don't want to worship from afar; draw me near to where You are."

This should be the heartfelt prayer of every child of God, for without His presence, we are nothing. It is only when we abide in His presence that our spirits are renewed, our purposes are aligned, and our lives bear the sweet savor of genuine worship. As Jesus declared in John

15:4-5,

> *"Abide in me, and I in you. As the branch cannot bear fruit by itself, unless it abides in the vine, neither can you, unless you abide in me. I am the vine, you are the branches. Whoever abides in me and I in him, he it is that bears much fruit; for apart from me you can do nothing."*

Let this truth be the foundation upon which we build our daily altars, ensuring that every moment of communion draws us closer to the heart of God and empowers us to live out His divine purpose.

OUTLINE FOR A DAILY COMMUNION

1. Preparation Time

To have a good devotion time, you need to prepare yourself physically, mentally, emotionally, and spiritually. The physical preparation is the easiest. Find a comfortable location where you will not be distracted, and gather any resources you might need. I always have my Bible, paper, and a pen at hand, while others may choose to play worship music as they commence their time with the Lord. Once you've chosen the right place and assembled your materials, settle into a position that enables you to focus fully on God—whether that means kneeling, walking slowly, or simply sitting in quiet reflection. The main purpose is to meet with God and concentrate on His presence. Some may approach prayer time as though they are negotiating a deal, but true communion with God demands reverence and sincerity. In addition to physically distancing yourself from distractions like a busy household or crowded environment, you must commit this time to the Lord in heartfelt prayer. It is only through such deliberate preparation that the Holy Spirit can draw you closer to Him, ensuring that your daily communion becomes a transformative experience.

2. Waiting Time

"Be still, and know that I am God" (Psalm 46:10).

When you enter into God's presence, it is essential to allow for a time of waiting—a time of stillness and reflection. In the example of Moses, though he had an appointment with the Lord, God did not begin to speak to him until the seventh day. This waiting period was not wasted time; it was a sacred interval during which Moses prepared his heart, cleared his mind, and attuned his spirit to receive divine revelation. In our busy lives, the concept of waiting may seem counterintuitive, but it is precisely during these quiet moments that God speaks most clearly. The waiting time is an opportunity to let go of the noise and chaos around you, to settle into a state of deep stillness where only God's voice remains. During this period, you may find that your thoughts gradually align with His, and what initially seemed like silence becomes filled with spiritual insights. Cultivate this waiting time deliberately—it is a crucial component of your daily communion that enables you to hear the soft, gentle whispers of the Holy Spirit, guiding you on your journey and ensuring that your soul is nourished by His presence.

3. Confession

"If I regard iniquity in my heart, the Lord will not hear me"

(Psalm 66:18).

Confession is a fundamental step in our daily communion with God. We must come before Him with complete honesty, acknowledging our weaknesses and sins, for nothing is hidden from His sight. The promise of forgiveness is found in, "If we confess our sins, He is faithful and just to forgive us our sins, and to cleanse us from all unrighteousness" (I John 1:9). Concealing our sins only serves to create spiritual blockages, hindering the flow of God's blessings. As Proverbs 28:13 teaches, covering up our transgressions prevents us from experiencing true prosperity. It is only by laying our sins bare before the Lord, trusting in the cleansing power of Jesus' blood, that we receive forgiveness. Open up your heart sincerely and allow the Holy Spirit to reveal any hidden areas of sin. In doing so, you make space for healing, restoration, and a renewed intimacy with God. Your confession is not merely an admission of guilt—it is an invitation for God to work in you, to redeem, and to restore you fully to His grace.

4. Meditation Time

I encourage you to dedicate at least two minutes to pray to the Lord about a specific piece of His Word you wish to study, inviting Him to reveal His mind to you through it. This period of meditation is vital in sharpening your prayer life, as the Holy Spirit guides you to address specific issues that may be weighing on your heart. Write down the insights and concerns that arise, creating a roadmap for your prayer. This intentional practice of meditation helps clear the clutter of daily thoughts and focuses your mind on God's truths. As you meditate on His Word, you begin to uncover patterns, hidden lessons, and areas of your life that need transformation. This quiet reflection is not simply an intellectual exercise—it is an act of spiritual listening, where you open your heart to God's voice. By taking the time to meditate deliberately, you allow His wisdom to permeate your thoughts and direct your actions, ensuring that the issues that have long troubled your mind are addressed with divine clarity. This practice not only deepens your understanding of Scripture but also strengthens your relationship with the Lord, making your time at the altar a wellspring of spiritual renewal.

5. Intercession Time

Likewise, the Spirit helps with our infirmities: for we do not know what we should pray for, but the Spirit Himself intercedes for us with groanings that cannot be uttered (Romans 8:26-27). Intercession is among the most challenging yet essential forms of prayer—it requires us to stand in the gap for others, praying earnestly on their behalf. When you intercede, you act as a channel for God's mercy and intervention, lifting the burdens of others before Him. It is an act of love that demands empathy, patience, and a willingness to surrender your own concerns for the sake of those around you. Effective intercession involves not just reciting petitions, but engaging with the Holy Spirit to discern the deepest needs of those for whom you are praying. As you intercede, allow your heart to be filled with compassion and your mind to be aligned with God's will. This practice transforms your perspective, reminding you that every breath you take is connected to the wellbeing of others. The fulfillment of our lives is intricately linked to our willingness to help and support one another through prayer. As you intercede, you build a spiritual bridge that connects the pain and hopes of those in need with the boundless grace of God. The more you immerse yourself in intercession, the deeper your own faith grows, and the more potent your testimony becomes as a believer in Christ.

6. Petition Time

As individuals, we all have personal needs that must be met, and sometimes we face spiritual warfare that must be overcome. Petition time is the moment when you confidently approach the Lord and ask Him, with unwavering faith, for what you need. Jesus instructs us, "Have faith in God. For truly I say to you, whoever says to this mountain, 'Be taken up and thrown into the sea,' and does not doubt in his heart but believes that what he says will come to pass, it will be done for him" (Mark 11:22-24). This command reminds us that our petition time is not a moment for mere requests, but for engaging with God's power. Consistently walking in the pattern of daily devotion ensures that you are heard before you even call out, as Isaiah 65:24 promises, "Before they call, I will answer; and while they are yet speaking, I will hear." By trusting in God's timing and power, you can boldly bring your requests before Him, knowing that He is both willing and able to provide. Your petitions become a declaration of faith that aligns your heart with His divine purpose, empowering you to overcome every challenge.

7. Faith/Changing

When we open our hearts to Him and patiently wait for His response,

God speaks to us about the matters we have entrusted to Him in prayer, as well as those we may have overlooked but are of divine interest. When we pray, God not only listens but also responds—often filling our hearts with praise, thanksgiving, and a testimony of His faithfulness. As we experience His transformative touch, our lives undergo a profound change. The act of prayer leads to a renewal of faith that empowers us to live out His will with courage and conviction. This process of transformation is continuous; every day, as we abide in His presence, we grow more in our understanding of His ways and become more effective instruments for His kingdom. In the midst of our trials, we discover that God's voice brings clarity, hope, and direction. It is through such intimate communion with Him that our character is shaped and our destiny is revealed. Each answered prayer reaffirms our trust in His unfailing love, urging us to press on and to be living testimonies of His grace and mercy.

SABBATH OR WEEKLY ALTAR

The concept of dedicating a specific time each week for communion with the Lord is deeply rooted in biblical tradition. Under the Old Covenant, special sacrifices were prescribed for the Sabbath, ensuring that this day was set apart for holy encounter and worship. For instance, Numbers 28:9-10 states:

> *"And on the sabbath day, two lambs of the first year without spot, and two tenth deals of flour for a meat offering, mingled with oil, and the drink offering thereof: This is the burnt offering of every sabbath, beside the continual burnt offering,*

and his drink offering."

In Moses' time, when worship was administered under the veil of the tabernacle, this practice was an integral part of Israel's religious observance. Apart from the daily offerings, there was a dedicated Sabbath sacrifice and a distinct time for communion with the Lord. If the Israelites typically met with God for about thirty minutes each day, they likely enjoyed an additional hour on the Sabbath—a period that allowed for deeper focus, reflection, and spiritual renewal.

Today, there is no reason why a similar pattern of weekly offerings on the Lord's Day cannot continue under the new covenant. In fact, many believers would argue that the time spent with the Lord on weekends should be even more enriching than on ordinary weekdays. This special time with the Holy Spirit should be free from distractions—unlike larger church gatherings or night vigils, which, while important for communal fellowship, may not always offer the quiet, undisturbed space necessary for deep personal communion with God.

Establishing a weekly altar involves intentional planning and discipline. It is one thing to resolve, "I want to spend more time with the Lord," and quite another for external circumstances or even the enemy to dictate how your day unfolds, thereby disrupting the communion you have so diligently prepared for. True spiritual renewal requires that you set aside dedicated time that is free from interruptions—a time when you can fully engage in prayer, meditation on Scripture, and personal reflection.

John C. Maxwell, in his book *Partners in Prayer*, shared how he observed a quiet time at 1:00 p.m. every day during college and even after marriage. That consistent hour in the presence of the Lord laid the foundation for his ministry, which continues to influence countless lives today. Like Maxwell, you too need to deliberately carve out time on the Sabbath—or your designated day—to deepen your relationship with God.

In our modern, fast-paced world, setting aside this sacred time is both a challenge and a blessing. It requires you to resist the temptation to fill every moment with busyness, choosing instead to prioritize spiritual nourishment. The weekly altar is more than just a routine; it is a divine invitation to experience God's presence, to refresh your spirit, and to align your heart with His will. When you commit to this practice, you invite the transformative power of the Holy Spirit into your life, ensuring that you remain steadfast and fruitful in your walk with the Lord.

MONTHLY DEVOTIONAL ALTARS

The special prayer meetings held in churches on the first day of the month—or on a designated day each month—find their roots in the instructions given to Moses during Old Testament times. In addition to the Sabbath's additional offering, the people of Israel were commanded to offer a special sacrifice on the first day of each month. This monthly ritual served as a tangible reminder of their covenant with the Lord and a regular opportunity to re-enact their commitment through sacrificial offerings.

Consider Numbers 28:11-15, which states:

> *"And in the beginnings of your months ye shall offer a burnt*
> *offering unto the LORD; two young bullocks, and one ram,*
> *seven lambs of the first year without spot; And three tenth*
> *deals of flour for a meat offering, mingled with oil, for one*
> *bullock; and two tenth deals of flour for a meat offering,*
> *mingled with oil, for one ram; And a several tenth deal of flour*
> *mingled with oil for a meat offering unto one lamb; for a burnt*
> *offering of a sweet savour, a sacrifice made by fire unto the*
> *LORD. And their drink offerings shall be half an hin of wine*
> *unto a bullock, and the third part of an hin unto a ram, and a*
> *fourth part of an hin unto a lamb: this is the burnt offering of*
> *every month throughout the months of the year. And one kid*
> *of the goats for a sin offering unto the LORD shall be offered,*
> *beside the continual burnt offering, and his drink offering."*

This detailed prescription for the monthly offerings was more than a mere ritual—it was a reenactment of the covenant between God and His people. By observing these offerings, the Israelites regularly reminded themselves of their dependence on God and their commitment to live according to His law. They were encouraged not to rush into a new month without first seeking divine guidance for the days ahead. The same principle can be applied in our lives today. We, too, can set aside dedicated time at the beginning of each month—whether through personal prayer, meditation, or small group meetings—to seek God's direction and recommit ourselves to His purposes. Moreover, this practice can be extended to quarterly, midyear, and even yearly intervals, creating a consistent rhythm of renewal and spiritual growth.

Reflecting on my own experience, I recall a time when I led the prayer band at my church. Every quarter, I deliberately set aside three or four days to fast and pray, creating a sacred space to re-enact my covenant with God. This intentional period of withdrawal from the busyness of daily life allowed me to commune deeply with the Lord, and I firmly believe that it prepared the way for many of the blessings and opportunities God has since committed to my hands. During those days, I not only experienced personal renewal but also gained clarity about God's direction for my life. It was as though every fasting period cleared away the clutter of my thoughts, leaving me receptive to the divine voice and the gentle promptings of the Holy Spirit.

In our modern context, maintaining a monthly altar of devotion can serve as a powerful tool for spiritual discipline. Rather than simply following a routine, we are invited to see these times as opportunities to align our hearts with God's will, to set intentional goals for the coming month, and to reflect on His faithfulness. Whether you choose to observe this time alone in personal quietness or with your family in a collective setting, it is important to create an environment free from distractions. Let your space be a sanctuary where you can experience genuine intimacy with the Lord—a time to read Scripture, to meditate on His promises, and to pray for guidance and strength.

This way, you invite God's presence to permeate every area of your life, ensuring that as each new month begins, you step forward with a renewed spirit and a clear sense of purpose. The practice of dedicating specific times for communion is not merely an Old Testament tradition; it is a timeless invitation to encounter God in a way that transforms our lives. As you set aside this sacred time each month, may you experience the profound peace and direction that come from aligning your life with the divine rhythm established by God Himself.

Questions for Reflection

1. How do you (or can you) make sure that you are communing alone with God each day? What needs changed? What needs improved?

2. How do you include confession in your communion time with God? If you aren't, what is holding you back?

3. What is your system to regularly intercede in prayer for others? How can you improve it?

4. Are you stepping out in faith with your petitions to God? What can you ask Him for now, believing that with Him, all things are possible?

5. List some ideas to start incorporating weekly, monthly, or other occasions for altar times with God:

CHAPTER 8

HOME ALTARS

COUPLE ALTAR

L ike the old African adage goes, "He that is walking in a direction does not see what happens behind his head." This timeless wisdom reminds us of the importance for couples to vigilantly guard their spiritual journey together. In today's world, it is essential that couples closely monitor their lives and consistently pray for one another, ensuring that their relationship remains firmly guided by God rather than by external influences. More than that, couples must intentionally set aside time to commune with the Lord together—to listen to His voice, to receive His direction as one, and to share the individual burdens they bring before Him. True unity in marriage is achieved when both partners actively seek divine guidance, allowing their hearts and minds to align with God's will.

Consider the profound truth found in Ecclesiastes 4:8-12:

> *"There is one alone, and there is not a second: yea, he hath neither child nor brother: yet is there no end of all his labour; neither is his eye satisfied with riches; neither saith he, 'For whom do I labour, and bereave my soul of good?' This is also vanity, yea, it is a sore travail. Two are better than one;*

because they have a good reward for their labour. For if they fall, the one will lift up his fellow: but woe to him that is alone when he falleth; for he hath not another to help him up. Again, if two lie together, then they have heat: but how can one be warm alone? And if one prevail against him, two shall withstand him; and a threefold cord is not quickly broken."

These verses underscore that a united couple is stronger and more resilient than an individual facing life's challenges alone. When couples pray together and build a personal altar of worship in their home, they create a sacred space where love, support, and divine guidance flourish. This spiritual foundation is critical not only for overcoming challenges but also for nurturing a deep, lasting relationship.

As families grow and children come along, the couple's personal communion altar may be strained. Without careful attention, the sacred bond can weaken, making room for discord and external influence. The harsh reality is that every Christian couple must intentionally set aside time to be alone together, even amid a packed schedule, to align their hearts with God's mind. Too often, I have heard couples express negative opinions about each other to co-workers, friends, or family members. Such behavior usually stems from a lack of spiritual unity—their hearts are not in sync because they have not cultivated a shared communion with the Lord. When couples do not pray together, they risk drifting apart, and their relationship can suffer irreparable damage. Consistent, intentional communion not only deepens their bond but also fortifies their marriage against the challenges of life.

In essence, the altar that couples build in their homes is a vital place of unity and strength. It is a space where both partners can express love, lay aside pride, and seek the divine guidance necessary for a thriving relationship. As you invest in this sacred practice, may your home be transformed into a sanctuary of mutual respect, spiritual growth, and unwavering commitment to God.

FAMILY ALTAR

As the name implies, a family altar involves a dedicated space and time set aside for the entire household—fathers, mothers, children, relatives, and dependents—to come together in communion with the Lord. Unlike a personal altar, which is often a private time of quiet devotion, the family altar is a collective expression of faith. Every morning or evening, families gather to sing songs, read from the Bible, and, if time permits, share insights from God's Word before starting their day or winding down. This practice is not merely a routine; it is a sacred appointment designed to align the hearts of each family member with God's purposes. While individual worship is important, the strength of a household is amplified when its members deliberately choose to commune with the Lord together.

I also encourage families to occasionally step away from their usual home setting and arrange to meet in a designated location where distractions are minimized—a quiet retreat, a resort center, or any space conducive to focused prayer and worship. The children of Israel practiced a similar discipline when they journeyed to Jerusalem for worship, leaving behind everyday distractions to fully engage with God. By removing themselves from the routine environment, families can experience a deeper, undisturbed level of communion that rejuvenates their spirit and strengthens their unity. This intentional separation from daily chaos allows them to experience God's presence in a more profound and transformative way.

Spiritual wisdom teaches that every Christian home should establish a family altar. This is not a suggestion for non-Christian households, which must first embrace Christ before they can participate in true worship. For Christian families, however, the family altar is essential. Ask yourself: Is worshiping together the most important function in your family? Is there anything more vital, more enduring, and more significant than coming together daily as a family to honor and worship the Lord? The practice of gathering in unity serves as the foundation of your spiritual home, setting the tone for every other aspect of your life.

Regrettably, many families today inadvertently raise an altar of neglect when it comes to worshiping together at home. The writer of Hebrews asks a sobering question: "How shall we escape if we neglect so great salvation...?" (Hebrews 2:3). Neglect, in this context, refers to failing to nurture our salvation by overlooking the importance of consistent, communal worship. The Apostle Paul reinforces this point in 1 Timothy 5:8, stating, "But if any provide not for his own, and especially for those of his own house, he hath denied the faith, and is worse than an infidel." If raising an altar of neglect in the realm of material provisions is so grievous, how much more grievous is it to neglect the spiritual nourishment that comes from daily worship? Ignoring the family altar not only stunts individual spiritual growth but also weakens the bond that should unite the household under God's protection.

While private devotion is commendable, it can never substitute for the unique benefits derived from family worship. The family altar must be firmly established in the hearts of the parents, who are the spiritual leaders in the home. They set the tone for how worship is experienced, ensuring that the practice becomes a major project in the family's life. Remember, the most important church is the church in your house. A family that worships together is better equipped to gather for corporate worship in the broader church community. The home and the church are mutually supportive, but the journey of worship begins at home. Through consistent family worship, every member grows in faith, and the collective strength of the household becomes a beacon of hope and unity.

Establishing a family altar is not a ritual. On the contrary, it is an ongoing commitment to nurturing a relationship with God together as a family. This altar fosters an environment where love, mutual support, and spiritual growth can thrive. When families prioritize the altar of worship, they honor God and create a legacy of faith that their children can imbibe and pass on to the next generations. I invite us to commit to making the family altar a central part of our daily routine. This is how the foundation of a strong, unified home is built on the eternal truths of God's Word.

The family altar may not guarantee a problem-free existence, but it ensures a place of refuge and a sanctuary for sharing the burdens and joys of family life. When a family gathers in worship, children hear their names spoken with heartfelt concern at the feet of the Heavenly Father, and parents experience the unique blessing of hearing their children pray for them in ways that no one else can. This sacred practice is essential for nurturing deep, spiritual connections within the household. The family altar is more than a daily routine—it is a powerful institution that instills values, reinforces bonds, and sets the spiritual foundation for every member of the family. Through regular family worship, the entire household is drawn closer to God, and His presence permeates every aspect of their lives.

1. Exalting the Word of God in the Home

Family worship provides a dynamic platform for exalting the Word of God within the home. The Bible, being given by the very hand of God, deserves to be held in the highest regard. As II Timothy 3:16-17 declares,

> *"All Scripture is given by inspiration of God, and is profitable for doctrine, for reproof, for correction, for instruction in righteousness: that the man of God may be perfect, thoroughly furnished unto all good works."*

Moreover, Romans 15:4 teaches that

> *"For whatsoever things were written aforetime were written for our learning, that we through patience and comfort of the scriptures might have hope."*

The Bible's role as an unerring guide is further highlighted in Proverbs 6:23,

> *"For the commandment is a lamp; and the law is light; and reproofs of instruction are the way of life."*

When families gather around the family altar, they study and discuss God's Word and allow the Word to shape their character and influence their decisions. This regular engagement with Scripture cultivates an environment where faith in God can grow, providing a strong foundation for making wise choices in everyday life and navigating life's difficult terrain. A home that exalts the Word of God, every member learns to cherish and live by God's truth. And the light of God's Word continues to shine brightly from one generation to another.

2. Uniting the Family in Prayer

Family worship is also a vital means by which the entire household can come together in prayer. The family altar often becomes the venue for prayers that address personal struggles, familial challenges, and communal needs—prayers that might be too intimate to share in a public setting. This fits the type of prayer mentioned in Matthew 6:6,

> *"But thou, when thou prayest, enter into thy closet, and when thou hast shut thy door, pray to thy Father which is in secret; and thy Father which seeth in secret shall reward thee openly."*

This style of private, heartfelt prayer is crucial for maintaining a strong connection with God. It is at the family altar that the doors are closed to outside distractions, creating a safe space for each family member to pour out their hearts to God.

Yet, when outsiders are around (maybe via visitation), families must continue to raise this family altar. For example, Daniel knew someone was watching and he **"prayed, and gave thanks before his God, as he did aforetime"** (Daniel 6:10). When families engage in unified prayer, they build a spiritual bond that not only lifts individual burdens but also strengthens the entire family unit. The act of interceding for one another cultivates empathy, mutual support, and resilience, enabling the family to weather any storm with a unified spirit of hope and faith.

3. Setting an Example for Others

Diligently practicing the family altar sets a powerful example for the world. As Paul writes in II Corinthians 3:2, "Ye are our epistle written in our hearts, known and read of all men." Our lives become a living testament to the life-changing power of God's love when we consistently gather in worship as a family. Jesus encouraged us in Matthew 5:16 to "Let your light so shine before men, that they may see your good works, and glorify your Father which is in heaven." When a family regularly worships together, it sends a clear message to others that their lives have been transformed by Christ. Furthermore, Paul explains in Romans 6:4, "Therefore we are buried with him by baptism into death: that like as Christ was raised up from the dead by the glory of the Father, even so we also should walk in newness of life." This renewal, experienced through the discipline of family worship, strengthens the family internally and also serves as an example to others, inspiring them to seek a similar deep, communal relationship with God. In a world that often seems fragmented and divided, the family altar becomes a strong, unifying force, pointing to the power of collective faith and the influence of a household anchored in God.

4. Teaching Children Their Duty to God

One of the most significant benefits of the family altar is its role in teaching children their duty to God. In a Christian home, the family altar is the primary environment where young hearts are introduced to spiritual truths. As Ecclesiastes 12:1 advises, "Remember now thy Creator in the days of thy youth," it is important to instill love for God early in life. In addition, Proverbs 24:21 instructs, "My son, fear thou the Lord…," and Deuteronomy 30:2 exhorts parents to ensure that both they and their children obey the commands of God with all their heart and soul. When children observe their parents engaging in regular worship and prayer, they internalize these practices, learning by example the value of reverence and obedience. This daily exposure to the discipline of family worship becomes a foundation for a lifelong commitment to God, shaping their character and influencing their decisions well into adulthood. Through the family altar, children develop a personal relationship with God, equipping them with the spiritual resilience needed to triumph in life.

5. Teaching Children Their Duty to Parent

Equally important is the role of the family altar in teaching children about their responsibilities toward their parents. The Bible instructs us to honor our father and mother, as seen in Exodus 20:12, "Honour thy father and thy mother: that thy days may be long upon the land which the LORD thy God giveth thee." In Ephesians 6:1-2, Paul emphasizes, "Children, obey your parents in the Lord: for this is right. Honor thy father and mother; which is the first commandment with promise." When families gather together to worship, children witness firsthand the respect and honor with which their parents approach God. This not only reinforces the importance of filial piety but also helps children understand their own role in caring for and supporting their parents. Additionally, I Timothy 5:4 instructs that widows with children or nephews should first learn to exhibit piety at home and to repay their parents, highlighting the value of nurturing and honoring family relationships. The practice of family worship thus becomes an opportunity for parents to pass on essential values and for children to learn the virtues of respect, responsibility, and love. These lessons, taught in regular communion with God, have lasting impacts on the lives of children.

6. Winning Children to Christ

Another vital aspect of the family altar is its role in leading children to Christ. The family altar is a natural setting for parents to introduce their children to the ways of the Lord. Deuteronomy 31:12 instructs, "Gather the people together, men, and women, and children, and thy stranger that is within thy gates, that they may hear, and that they may learn, and fear the LORD your God, and observe to do all the words of this law." This call to gather underscores the importance of a shared spiritual experience where children are exposed to the foundational truths of the Gospel. Moreover, Ephesians 2:8 tells us that "For by Grace are ye saved through faith; and that not of yourselves: it is the gift of God." Through regular family worship, children learn that salvation is a gift, not something earned, and that a relationship with Christ is the most valuable treasure of all. Jesus' gentle invitation in Mark 10:14-16—"Suffer little children to come unto me, and forbid them not: for of such is the kingdom of God"—further points to the importance of drawing children into the fold of God. When the family altar is a central part of a household, children are allowed to experience the love of God directly, setting the stage for a lifelong commitment to His teachings.

7. Growing in Grace through the Family Altar

Finally, the family altar is a means by which Christians can grow in grace. II Peter 3:18 exhorts us, "But grow in grace, and in the knowledge of our Lord and Saviour Jesus Christ," while II Timothy 2:1 encourages, "Thou therefore, my son, be strong in the grace that is in Christ Jesus." Daily reading of the Scriptures and consistent prayer practice are essential for strengthening our inner spiritual lives. Although many lament that children do not hear Bible readings and prayers at school, I often wonder if those same children receive adequate spiritual nourishment at home. The responsibility of Christian education ultimately rests on the church—a community composed of families that ideally practice worship seven days a week with established family altars. When the home becomes a hub of daily worship, it nurtures individual spiritual growth and builds a robust foundation for the broader community. The family altar transforms the home into a sanctuary of divine fellowship, where God's presence is experienced continuously, His Word is cherished, and His love is actively shared.

Therefore, the family altar is not simply an optional ritual. It is a vital discipline that anchors a Christian home in the love and truth of God. It provides a haven for sharing burdens, reinforces the exaltation of God's Word, unifies the family in prayer, and serves as a powerful witness to the world. Through consistent family worship, parents can instill essential values, teach children their duties to God and to their parents, and even lead them to Christ. Furthermore, the family altar is instrumental in helping every member grow in grace. As we commit to making the family altar a central practice in our lives, we are building a legacy of faith, unity, and divine guidance that endures for generations, ultimately setting the stage for societal transformation.

The cure for juvenile delinquency must begin before children are born. It starts in the hearts of young people who turn away from a life solely centered on the marriage altar and instead establish a family altar. The family altar is a dedicated space where the entire household—parents, children, relatives, and dependents—commits to daily communion with the Lord. It is a place where the heart is quieted, and our purposes are realigned to live out the covenant we made with God when we became Christians and when we entered into marriage. When family worship is a daily practice, the dedication of one's children is not reduced to a mere formality or empty ritual; it becomes the heartfelt passing on of spiritual values and life experiences from one generation to the next, a true heart-to-heart and soul-to-soul encounter with God's love.

Consider the example of the Recabites, a family renowned for their strict adherence to a divine command.

> *Go to the settlement where the families of the Recabites live, and invite them to the LORD's Temple. Take them into one of the inner rooms, and offer them some wine." So I went to see Jaazaniah, son of Jeremiah and grandson of Habazziniah, and all his brothers and sons—representing all the Recabite families. I took them to the Temple, and we went into the room assigned to the sons of Hanan son of Igdaliah, a man of God. This room was located next to the one used by the Temple officials, directly above the room of Maaseiah son of Shallum, the Temple gatekeeper. I set cups and jugs of wine before them and invited them to have a drink, but they refused. "No," they said, "we don't drink wine, because our ancestor Jehonadab son of Recab gave us this command: 'You and your descendants must never drink wine* (Jeremiah 35:2-6, NLT).

The Recabites continually reminded themselves at the altar of their commitment to abstain from wine. Even when an anointed person urged them to partake, they stood firm, preserving the sacred testimony passed down through generations. This testifies to the fact that when you uphold the traditions of your family altar, your children will follow suit.

While the family altar may not eliminate all life's problems, it provides a sanctuary of faith, trust, and comfort. There is no substitute for a family that prays together and worships God within the safe walls of their home. I highly recommend establishing a family altar, for truly, the family that prays together stays together.

Questions for Reflection

1. If you're married, how and when can you establish altar time together? If you already have one, how can you improve and expand it?

2. If you have children, how and when can you establish altar time together? If you already have one, how can you improve and expand it?

3. In what ways are you exalting the Word of God in your home? How can you enhance or increase this?

4. When and how often does your family pray together? How can you add more prayer in your home?

5. How does your family shine Christ's light on others? In what ways can you witness to and serve others this week together? This month? This year?

CHAPTER 9

ALTARS OF AFFLICTION

I do not suppose that this book is solely a systematic attempt to examine the altars that emerged in every fourteenth generation. Rather, its greater purpose is to call our attention, as believers, to evaluate our own lives, families, and the generation to which we belong. Consequently, we now turn our focus to the afflictions that hinder our communion with the Lord.

Abu Bako, in his book *Praying Through the Gates of Time*, explained that the foundation of any kingdom consists of its GATES, ALTARS, and COVENANTS. To effectively dismantle any stronghold, one must begin at its very foundation. In light of this, we are compelled to scrutinize the altars that have existed in our family lineages before our time and to break their hold. Recall the passage in Exodus 20:4-6: if altars were raised for God, He would bestow mercy upon a thousand generations; however, if they were erected in opposition to Him, He would visit iniquity upon the third and fourth generations.

A sister in Christ once ran to a man of God for assistance regarding her father's failing investment. She revealed that her great-grandfather had been a powerful occultist, frequently sacrificing chickens at the village's pagan shrine whenever he was consulted for spiritual guidance. By the time missionaries arrived in their village, her great-grandfather had long passed away, and his son had abandoned the priestly role to the pagan deity, choosing instead to attend church with his children, one of whom was her father.

After retiring from the civil service, her father decided to invest his savings in a venture promising a good return—he chose the poultry business. Unaware of the dark history of the land, which had once served as the site for sacrificial rites at the pagan shrine, he believed it to be the ideal location for his poultry farm. In a short period, he constructed pens and began stocking the area with birds intended for meat production. Yet, whenever the birds neared maturity and the time for slaughter approached, thousands would suddenly die. This tragic cycle repeated several times until his entire savings were depleted. It was at that desperate moment that his daughter sought the help of the man of God. Through prayer, they discovered that the land had been dedicated to their ancestral family gods, and as a result, her father was suffering for the sins of his forefathers, just as the Scriptures forewarn.

While God's Word affirms that the punishment for sin may extend to future generations, it equally promises that God shows favor to those who love Him and keep His commandments (Exodus 20:5-6). In the case of this family, who were suffering under the weight of ancestral sin, the revelation that their land had once been used for idolatrous purposes necessitated immediate action. Upon learning this truth, they understood that they must adhere to Biblical instructions to reverse the curse:

A) Declare and devote the property's purpose to the Lord.

Declaring and devoting a property's purpose to the Lord means sanctifying that space and transforming its identity from one marked by dark practices into a place of divine favor. As stated in Leviticus 27:28,

"Every devoted offering is most holy to the Lord."

This act is not merely symbolic; it is a powerful declaration that reclaims the land for God's glory. By proclaiming its sanctity, we consciously reject any lingering influences of its former, ungodly use, and invite God's presence to dwell there. The property is thus redefined—a once defiled space becomes a beacon of hope and divine mercy – and its history is rewritten from a site of dark practices to one of divine favor. This act of faith honors the Lord and also blesses future generations, turning a troubled history into a legacy of faith and righteousness. In dedicating the property to God, we affirm that every piece of land can be redeemed and repurposed for God's eternal glory.

B) Dedicate the land to its intended purpose.

The earth belongs to God and is meant to serve His purposes. No place was ever meant to function as an altar to idols. After the godless Chaldeans robbed and destroyed God's holy temple, the Israelites returned to that very site and rebuilt the temple where so much evil had once taken place, thus restoring the land to its intended purpose— a sacred space for worshiping the Most High God. Ezra 6:16 recounts, "And the people of Israel, the priests and the Levites, and the rest of the returned exiles, celebrated the dedication of this house of God with joy."

C) Dedicate resources obtained from ungodly sources to the Lord.
An example of this is found when David's army defeated ungodly, idolatrous peoples such as the Moabites, who worshipped the false god Moab. 1 Chronicles 26:27 notes, "From spoil won in battles they dedicated gifts for the maintenance of the house of the Lord." This act of redirection symbolizes reclaiming what once belonged to darkness and restoring it for the glory of God.

There isn't a single verse that explicitly states, "Dedicate a place of evil to God's purpose," yet the concept is vividly illustrated in Genesis 50:20. In that passage, Joseph tells his brothers, "But as for you, you meant evil against me; but God meant it for good, in order to bring it about as it is this day, to save many people alive" (NKJV). This declaration emphasizes that God is capable of transforming even the most corrupted situations and spaces for His good purposes, provided that we surrender them to Him and act in accordance with His will. Romans 12:21 reinforces this by urging, "Do not be overcome by evil, but overcome evil with good" (NKJV).

Beloved, consider the altars raised in the last fourteenth generation of your lineage. Are these altars invoking the mercy of God, or do they call forth His wrath? To prevent a life of perpetual struggle—constantly running like one beating the air—you must examine and close those gates of affliction that the enemy might have opened against your gloriously destined future. In their place, you need to open the unopened gates of favor that await you. Do not remain ignorant of spiritual matters. As 1 Peter 5:8 (NKJV) warns, "Be sober, be vigilant; because your adversary the devil walks about like a roaring lion, seeking whom he may devour."

It is crucial for every believer to assess the spiritual altars in our lineage. These altars may be subtle yet potent hindrances that affect our communion with the Lord, influencing our family's destiny for generations. We must be intentional about identifying and dismantling any altars that are contrary to God's will. Only by doing so can we experience the full blessing of a covenant relationship with God—a relationship that brings mercy, favor, and divine prosperity across all generations. Let us examine our spiritual heritage with discernment, purge the remnants of idolatry, and declare every possession and purpose for the Lord, so that we may fully inherit His blessings for a thousand generations.

BIBLICAL ALTARS OF AFFLICTION

Earlier in this chapter, at the beginning of the section on the altars of the fourteenth generation, I shared a story of a woman whose father had converted the ancestral shrine—an altar once dedicated to their forefathers—into a poultry farm. In doing so, the enemy exploited those very altars, raising an affliction that ultimately destroyed her business. This tragic example demonstrates the extreme lengths to which the enemy will go to secure and expand his territory.

There are millions of altars of various types, and these altars, along with their accompanying covenants, form a crucial part of the foundation of any kingdom. It is no wonder that when Abraham received the call to enter the Promised Land, he began raising altars at every significant juncture. Those altars served to prevent evil forces from establishing strongholds in those sacred places. The altars Abraham erected were intended to covenant the future kingship of Israel to God, as exemplified by the altar at Hebron. Just as altars serve as a place to contact and commune with the Almighty daily, so too have the devil and his hosts manipulated these sacred spaces to afflict people and even the children of God who are not vigilant. This underscores the urgent need for us to identify and silence these altars of affliction permanently.

Today, the gospel encounters many stumbling blocks when presented to both individuals and communities. As scripture tells us, while men were asleep, the enemy came and seized territories both physically and spiritually (Matthew 13:25). All he needed was to incite people against God by making them bow to idols. According to Exodus 20:1-6, such idolatrous acts naturally incurred the wrath of God.

Consider the account of Balaam. He instructed King Balak,

> *"Build me seven altars here, and prepare seven young bulls and seven rams for me to sacrifice."*

Balak obeyed these instructions, and together they sacrificed a young bull and a ram on each altar. Then Balaam said to Balak,

> *"Stand here by your burnt offerings, and I will go to see if the LORD will respond to me. Then I will relay whatever He reveals."*

Balaam ascended alone to the top of a bare hill, and it was there that God met with him. Balaam declared,

"I have prepared seven altars and have sacrificed a young bull and a ram on each one."

The LORD provided Balaam with a message for King Balak, instructing him to return and deliver this divine message. When Balaam returned, he found King Balak standing beside his burnt offerings with all the officials of Moab. The message delivered was as follows:

"Balak summoned me from Aram; the king of Moab brought me from the eastern hills. 'Come,' he said, 'curse Jacob for me! Come, announce Israel's doom.' But how can I curse those whom God has not cursed? How can I condemn those whom the LORD has not condemned? I see them from the cliff tops; I watch them from the hills. I see a people who live by themselves, set apart from other nations. Who can count Jacob's descendants, as numerous as the dust? Who can count even a fourth of Israel's people? Let me die as the righteous do; let my life end as theirs."

In response, King Balak demanded,

"What have you done to me? I brought you here to curse my enemies, and you have blessed them instead!"

To which Balaam replied, *"I will speak only the message that the LORD puts in my mouth."* (Numbers 23:1-12, NLT).

The phrase in verse 9b, *"I see a people who live by themselves, set apart from other nations,"* as rendered in the New Living Translation, indicates that they were distinct—greater, more powerful, and self-sufficient. They possessed all they needed because they were directly connected to the SOURCE of life, God, with whom they enjoyed uninterrupted communion as a nation before the enemy struck. Neighbors observed that they lived apart, without the need for alliances with other powers, because the altar of the Most Powerful was with them. No affliction, enchantment, or divination could stand against them (Numbers 23:23).

Balak, the Moabite king, along with his hired prophet Balaam, went so far as to sacrifice twenty-one young bulls and twenty-one rams on three strategically located altars at different times, all designed to launch a coordinated attack on the children of Israel.

They sharpened their tongues like swords, aiming their bitter words like arrows. They launched ambushes against the innocent, striking suddenly and without fear. They incited one another to commit evil and plotted in secrecy, asking, "*Who will ever notice?*" (Psalm 64:3-5, NLT).

Yet, all these efforts proved futile because Israel was on God's side, and God was on their side. Beloved, a person who does good should naturally not allow evil to invade their domain. As long as Israel adhered to the terms of God's covenant, they remained secure. However, any attempt to deviate from that covenant inevitably resulted in long-awaited afflictions in the form of curses overtaking them. This principle still holds today: when we remain obedient to God's Word, He prevents the enemy from prevailing over us.

The narrative shifted, however, between Numbers 23:9—when the people were distinct, supreme, and powerful above other nations—and Numbers 25:3, when they began to join themselves to Baalpeor. Initially, Israel recognized that they dwelled apart because of their unique relationship with God, but during that period they became entangled with Baalpeor. In the interim, Balaam counseled Balak in Numbers 22:21: "So Balaam rose in the morning, saddled his donkey, and went with the princes of Moab" (NKJV).

This counsel is echoed in Revelation 2:14, which states,

> *"But I have a few things against thee, because thou hast there them that hold the doctrine of Balaam, who taught Balak to cast a stumbling block before the children of Israel, to eat things sacrificed unto idols, and to commit fornication."*

Balaam, acting on Balak's behalf, instructed him in a method to lead the men of Israel into sin—by engaging in sexual immorality with Moabite women and by consuming food sacrificed to idols. As soon as they embraced these practices, the protective covering of God's favor was torn away, and affliction immediately set in. That day, before God's wrath was appeased, 24,000 people died.

ALTARS OF AFFLICTION TODAY

Affliction does not define the life of a Christian; however, suffering is not foreign to us because we are called not only to believe in Christ but also to suffer for His sake. "For it has been granted to you on behalf of Christ not only to believe in Him, but also to suffer for Him" (Philippians 1:29). Yet, suffering is different from affliction. The examination of Balaam's story and his dealings with Israel is truly an eye-opener. Forces beyond God's sovereign will sought to manipulate Israel and bring affliction upon them. Their objective was clear: to sever the divine connection and impose a lasting burden.

In many instances, the enemy transforms what should have been a season of refining suffering into a lifelong affliction. Today, there are countless altars of affliction—sites where the power of darkness is allowed to remain because they are not consecrated to the sacrificial Lamb of God, the Lord Jesus Christ. As the Scripture declares, "There is no judgment against anyone who believes in Him. But anyone who does not believe in Him has already been judged for not believing in God's one and only Son" (John 3:18, NLT). Such altars are effectively raising strange fires before God, reminiscent of the tragic example of Nadab and Abihu, the sons of Aaron, who offered unauthorized fire before the LORD.

Jesus has become our ultimate sacrifice, and it is solely through Him that we gain access to the Father. Yet today, there are prayer houses and churches that, instead of pointing believers to Christ, seem to seek diabolical power to draw men into their congregations. "But God's truth stands firm like a foundation stone with this inscription: 'The LORD knows those who are His,' and 'All who belong to the LORD must turn away from evil'" (II Timothy 2:19, NLT). God knows those who truly belong to Him, and at the right time, those who misuse His name will face judgment before the Most Holy God.

Every existing cult, regardless of its design, has its own altar—an altar dedicated to sacrificing to the devil, thereby afflicting the children of

God and undermining God's kingdom. These altars, though varied in form and practice, are designed to confuse and deceive believers in Christ regarding the true mastership of the spiritual realm. However, for those led by the Spirit of God, the workings of these altars become clear. As the apostle John admonishes, "Beloved, do not believe every spirit, but test the spirits to see whether they are from God, for many false prophets have gone out into the world. By this you know the Spirit of God: every spirit that confesses that Jesus Christ has come in the flesh is from God, and every spirit that does not confess Jesus is not from God" (I John 4:1).

Just as Balaam stood by Balak, the Moabite king, we too face priests and leaders who serve these demonic altars. Their primary target is none other than the Church of Christ. This is why the church must unite as a formidable force to expose and dismantle every scheme devised by the enemy to contaminate the hearts and minds of believers with false teaching, evil deeds, and blasphemy. As the Scripture warns, "They have forsaken the right way and gone astray, following the way of Balaam, the son of Beor, who loved the wages of unrighteousness" (II Peter 2:15, NKJV).

The call is clear: "Therefore, submit to God. Resist the devil, and he will flee from you. Draw near to God, and He will draw near to you. Cleanse your hands, you sinners; and purify your hearts, you double-minded" (James 4:7-8, NLT). Beloved, this is a summons for us to exalt the Lord by continually raising altars in worship, prayer, and thanksgiving. The profound impact of such devotion is that the devil and his agents will be driven out, while God is lifted high, drawing souls to Himself—especially those ensnared in a covenant with the enemy. The more altars we raise for the Lord, the more of the enemy's altars will be torn down around the world, and the greater the number of lives and territories will be claimed for the Kingdom of God.

Consider the Parable of the Ten Minas in Luke 19:11-27. As Jesus neared His death, He explained to His disciples that the Kingdom of God would not arrive immediately. He spoke of a nobleman who was going away and would return, instructing His servants, "Occupy till I come." This directive was not about negotiation or discussion—it was a clear command: go and do My work while I am absent. Part of that work involves winning territories, a task achievable only through the altars we raise in worship to the Lord.

Abraham raised altars in his time, and even today, his descendants hold onto the sacred sites where those altars once stood. Why not seize the opportunity to claim territories for the Lord? Some of these altars might need to be physically reclaimed after we secure our spiritual victories. Ultimately, winning is the very mind of God for us. As we engage in constant communion with Him and demolish the altars of affliction, we align ourselves with His divine plan for expansion and victory.

Let us therefore examine our own lives and the legacy of our lineage. Are there altars of affliction—those subtle, spiritual strongholds— that remain unchallenged? They may be hidden, yet their influence can disrupt our ability to fully experience God's favor. In our modern world, many believers are unaware of the spiritual battleground beneath them. We must remain vigilant, for the gates of affliction are often open to the enemy's advance. Our duty is to identify these areas, close those gates, and open the gates of favor that await us. Do not let ignorance prevail in spiritual matters. As 1 Peter 5:8 (NKJV) cautions, "Be sober, be vigilant; because your adversary the devil walks about like a roaring lion, seeking whom he may devour."

By actively confronting and dismantling these altars of affliction, we ensure that our lives are not held hostage by the sins of our forefathers or the deceptions of the enemy. Instead, we position ourselves to inherit the fullness of God's blessings—a heritage free from the curses of idolatry and spiritual bondage. In doing so, we honor the covenant established from the earliest generations and secure a legacy of righteousness for a thousand generations.

ALTARS OF AFFLICTION WITHIN

Witchcraft is, in many ways, another name for the inner afflictions that can plague a believer's life, and it is this very phenomenon that Balaam the prophet once exploited. He understood the most effective way to undermine his fellow man by advising an unbeliever on how to strike at the people of God. Although Balaam was not an Israelite, he possessed an uncanny knowledge of divine principles and knew precisely what could be done to weaken God's people from within. Even David, a man after God's own heart, was not spared; afflictions emerged within the very seat of his reign. These internal altars—spiritual strongholds built up from sin, deceit, and hidden agendas—serve as conduits through which the enemy sows discord and despair. They are not external forces alone; they reside deep within our homes, hearts, and relationships, ready to sabotage our communion with God. When such altars are allowed to persist, they not only hinder our spiritual growth but also obstruct the flow of God's blessings through our lives, ensuring that His purpose remains unfulfilled.

False witnesses also arise, bringing charges and slander that contaminate our souls.

> *"False witnesses did rise up: they laid to my charge things that I knew not. They rewarded me evil for good to the spoiling of my soul. But as for me, when they were sick, my clothing was sackcloth; I humbled my soul with fasting; and my prayer returned into mine own bosom. I behaved myself as though he had been my friend or brother: I bowed down heavily, as one that mourneth for his mother. But in mine adversity they rejoiced, and gathered themselves together: yea, the abjects gathered themselves together against me, and I knew it not; they did tear me, and ceased not"* (Psalm 35:11-15).

In these words, we see how betrayal and internal strife can form an altar of affliction that cuts deeply into one's spirit. When those close to us, sometimes even family members, engage in harmful gossip or sow seeds of discord, they inadvertently erect a spiritual barrier that distances us from God's healing presence.

Beloved, be vigilant and cautious. Never construct altars that bring affliction upon your fellow brethren through idle gossip, deliberate opposition to godly leadership, or persistent indulgence in sinful vices. Scripture reminds us, "...a man's enemies are the men of his own house" (Micah 7:6). This serves as a sobering warning that internal strife—often fueled by our own actions—can become the very means by which the enemy infiltrates and weakens our spiritual stronghold. We must guard our hearts and our homes, ensuring that the environment we create is one of unity, love, and mutual encouragement in the Lord.

Consider the case of a brother in Christ who proposed marriage to a sister in Christ, believing that it was God's will for him to spend his life with her. When she declined his proposal, instead of accepting her decision with grace, he chose to join forces in prayer with another brother. Together, they petitioned before the congregation that the sister, who had rejected him, would be cursed with disorder and misfortune until she relented. This act of spiritual manipulation represents a stark example of using the power of prayer and the altar to bring affliction on another person. Such behavior is contrary to the heart of true worship, which is meant to uplift and draw us closer to God. Instead of imposing our desires on others, we are called to seek the mind of God through sincere prayer, trusting that He will direct our paths in righteousness.

> *"Trust in the LORD with all thine heart; and lean not unto thine own understanding. In all thy ways acknowledge Him, and He shall direct thy paths"* (Proverbs 3:5-6).

The enemy delights in exploiting every opportunity to separate us from the love and unity that should characterize the body of Christ. When we engage in acts that build altars of affliction—whether through slander, selfish ambition, or misguided prayers—we open the door for the devil to operate unchecked within our midst. Such actions not only mar our personal relationships but also jeopardize the collective strength of the Church. It is essential that we reject any notion of using spiritual gifts as weapons against our fellow believers. Instead, let us use our gifts to edify one another, fostering an environment where God's mercy and favor can flourish.

The call to maintain a pure and undefiled communion with God requires us to examine our hearts and homes carefully. We must root out any spiritual altars built on sin or selfishness, ensuring that every act of worship, prayer, and fellowship is dedicated solely to glorifying the Lord. As we cleanse our spiritual environment, we pave the way for God's presence to fill every aspect of our lives. In doing so, we not only secure our own spiritual well-being but also contribute to the strengthening of the Church as a whole. The altars we build in our hearts must be holy places where the love of God is continually celebrated and where the enemy finds no foothold.

Let us remember that our ultimate mission is to become like Christ and advance the Kingdom of God by fostering unity and purity within our spiritual communities. When we rise above internal strife and embrace the liberating power of God's Word, we can dismantle the altars of affliction that seek to hold us back. In this way, our lives become living testimonies of His grace, drawing others into a deeper relationship with the One true God. May we be diligent in ensuring that our actions reflect His heart so that His light may shine through us and dispel every shadow of affliction in our lives.

DESTROYING STRANGE ALTARS

Judges 6:24-28

Then Gideon built an altar there unto the LORD, and called it Jehovahshalom: unto this day it is yet in Ophrah of the Abiezrites. And it came to pass the same night, that the LORD said unto him, Take thy father's young bullock, even the second bullock of seven years old, and throw down the altar of Baal that thy father hath, and cut down the grove that is by it: And build an altar unto the LORD thy God upon the top of this rock, in the ordered place, and take the second bullock, and offer a burnt sacrifice with the wood of the grove which thou shalt cut down. Then Gideon took ten men of his servants, and did as the LORD had said unto him: and so it was, because he feared his father's household, and the men of the city, that he could not do it by day, that he did it by night. And when the men of the city arose early in the morning, behold, the altar of Baal was cast down, and the grove was cut down that was by it, and the second bullock was offered upon the altar that was built.

The altars that Gideon's forefathers maintained led only to bondage, disorder, and suffering. While they labored, the Midianites consumed the fruits of their efforts, violating God's covenant that His people would not toil for others to reap the benefits. Their existence was in disarray until the Lord intervened. Dear reader, as you engage with this text, perhaps your circumstances mirror the tribulations the

Israelites endured until divine deliverance arrived. Now is your moment, but first, you must dismantle all altars of affliction erected against you. These may manifest as ancestral shrines still visited in your family home, objects placed within your residence or workplace that grant the enemy direct access to your life, or covenants made with the kingdom of darkness during times of ignorance about God— agreements that malevolent forces relentlessly exploit to afflict you from that point onward.

To address these challenges, begin by earnestly seeking the guidance of the Holy Spirit. Invite Him into your life through dedicated prayer and meditation, asking for the discernment to identify any hidden altars or ungodly influences that may be operating against you. This process requires a sincere commitment to self-examination and a willingness to confront uncomfortable truths about your spiritual environment. Set aside regular periods of quiet reflection, allowing God the space to reveal these spiritual strongholds to you. As you become aware of these altars, seek wisdom on the appropriate steps to dismantle them. This may involve renouncing past covenants, removing specific objects from your surroundings, or ceasing participation in certain practices. Remember, the journey to spiritual freedom is often gradual and necessitates patience, persistence, and unwavering faith in God's power to deliver and restore.

> *We use God's mighty weapons, not worldly weapons, to knock down the strongholds of human reasoning and to destroy false arguments. We destroy every proud obstacle that keeps people from knowing God. We capture their rebellious*

thoughts and teach them to obey Christ. And after you have become fully obedient, we will punish everyone who remains disobedient (II Corinthians 10:4-6, NLT).

The task of pulling down strongholds—those altars of affliction—and casting down imaginations and every high thing that seeks to exalt itself against the knowledge of God is, no doubt, a daunting one. But we're not in this alone. We can accomplish this through complete reliance on the Holy Spirit. Attempting to combat spiritual forces with physical means is futile and can lead to deeper entanglement with the very entities one seeks to overcome. Scripture reminds us that those who "wait upon the Lord shall renew their strength" (Isaiah 40:31). This waiting involves active trust and seeking divine instruction before engaging in spiritual battles. By positioning ourselves to hear from God and following His lead, we ensure that our efforts are not in vain and that victory is secured through His power, not our own. Therefore, prioritize seeking God's direction, immersing yourself in His Word, and cultivating a heart attuned to His voice. In doing so, you align yourself with His will and position yourself for triumph over the forces that seek to hinder your spiritual progress.

Consider the example of David, the renowned biblical figure who consistently sought the Lord's counsel before engaging in battle. Despite his experience as a warrior, David understood that each situation was unique and required divine guidance. He inquired of the Lord regarding the timing and strategy for each confrontation, demonstrating his dependence on God's wisdom rather than relying solely on past experiences or personal prowess. Similarly, the prophet

Elijah, during his confrontation with the prophets of Baal, acted explicitly according to God's instructions. In 1 Kings 18:36, Elijah prays, "Let it be known this day that You are God in Israel and I am Your servant, and that I have done all these things at Your word" (NKJV). These examples underscore the critical importance of seeking and adhering to God's direction in all endeavors, especially when confronting spiritual adversities and pulling down demonic altars. When we prioritize divine guidance, we acknowledge our limitations and invite God's omnipotence into our circumstances, ensuring that our actions are aligned with His will and empowered by His strength.

Questions for Reflection

1. Are you aware of evil practices or possessions in your family? Based on the information in this chapter, what can you do about them?

2. When has evil been used for good in your life? Record the blessings that God brought to your life.

3. What are you doing to pass down a heritage of righteousness to your family and future descendants?

4. In what ways do you believe Satan attacks you or your family? Read these scriptures to learn more about battling him: II Corinthians 10:35; James 4:7; Matthew 4:3-10.

5. Israel was a nation set apart. Are you living your life "set apart" for God at work? In your home? Do others know you are a Christian? What can you do to let others know that you live for God?

6. Israel sinned against God, so affliction set in. Do you know someone who has fallen away from God and into sin? List one or more names. Jot down some plans to reach out to them soon to share the love and forgiveness of God.

7. Are there some ungodly altars you are tolerating in your life or home? What actions can you take today to tear them down?

8. What are the biggest temptations you deal with? How can you resist the devil when he brings them your way? Write down a strategy for each temptation you face:

9. Jesus said in the parable to "occupy until I come." What kingdom work of His have you been delaying? What new work can you begin?

CHAPTER 10

THE ULTIMATE ALTAR

In my previous book, *The Fullness of His Covenant*, we explored the transformative power of the new covenant, established through Christ's sacrificial death and resurrection. This covenant secures a place for believers in heavenly realms with Christ, far above principalities and powers. Ephesians 2:6-7 (NLT)

> *For he raised us from the dead along with Christ and seated us with him in the heavenly realms because we are united with Christ Jesus. So God can point to us in all future ages as examples of the incredible wealth of his grace and kindness toward us, as shown in all he has done for us who are united with Christ Jesus.*

The crucifixion was accompanied by profound events—darkness covering the land, the temple curtain tearing, an earthquake, and the resurrection of the dead—confirming that something monumental had occurred. Long before Christ's sacrifice, Mount Moriah was the site of significant offerings—from Abraham's obedience to David's worship and Josiah's revival—foreshadowing the ultimate sacrifice that would deliver humanity from sin.

THE SPOT

Golgotha, the Place of the Skull where Jesus was crucified, is on Mount Moriah, approximately 300 meters from the temple in Jerusalem.[1] Hebrews 13:12 (NLT) states,

"So also Jesus suffered and died outside the city gates to make his people holy by means of his own blood."

This location carries deep significance. On this mount, Abraham and David offered sacrifices, Solomon built the temple, and Josiah renewed the covenant, hosting a celebrated Passover. Ultimately, the blood of Jesus was shed here, redeeming all humanity—God's intricate, deliberate plan.

Once sentenced to death, Jesus was led outside the city: "And they bring him unto the place Golgotha, which is, being interpreted, The place of a skull. And they gave him to drink wine mingled with myrrh: but he received it not. And when they had crucified him, they parted his garments, casting lots upon them, what every man should take" (Mark 15:22-24). Abraham's altar marked a beginning, and forty-two generations later, the ultimate altar was erected nearby. This was divine intention.

God's command in Exodus 20:4-6 reveals His heart for worship and obedience:

---

[1] Life Application Bible maps

Thou shalt not bow down thyself to them, nor serve them: for I the LORD thy God am a jealous God, visiting the iniquity of the fathers upon the children unto the third and fourth generation of them that hate me; And shewing mercy unto thousands of them that love me, and keep my commandments.

His desire for our worship is central—evident when the temple veil tore at Christ's death, signifying the end of sacrifices under the old covenant and the beginning of direct communion with God (Matthew 27:50-51).

And every priest stands ministering daily and offering repeatedly the same sacrifices, which can never take away sins. But this Man, after He had offered one sacrifice for sins forever, sat down at the right hand of God, from that time waiting till His enemies are made His footstool. For by one offering He has perfected forever those who are being sanctified. But the Holy Spirit also witnesses to us; for after He had said before, "This is the covenant that I will make with them after those days, says the Lord: I will put My laws into their hearts, and in their minds I will write them," then He adds, "Their sins and their lawless deeds I will remember no more." Now where there is remission of these, there is no longer an offering for sin (Hebrews 10:11-18, NKJV).

Satan's ultimate objective is to disrupt believers' communion with God—our spiritual lifeline. We must ask, "Am I truly communing with God?"

The point where all of these sacrifices took place which was first initiated by Abraham up until the time of Jesus as you would have understand is not intended to just bring you also to join the line and as some deem important visit Jerusalem and hopefully get to the wailing wall which would also fall around the perimeter of where all of these happened over these thousands of years. Instead to help you understand how intentional God is about always bringing his people to him whether they acknowledge him like David, submit to come to worship him through the law like Moses or get caught up in a revival fire like Josiah. One thing is constant: God would want his people to come to him at all times.

DAILY COMMUNION

Without Him, we are nothing; our spirit, left to wander without divine guidance, becomes lost in the chaos of a world that offers only temporary distractions. Our inner self, designed for communion with the Creator, craves a connection that only God can provide. Without His sustaining presence, we become like a ship adrift on stormy seas, lacking direction and vulnerable to every gust of wind. The human spirit is meant to flourish in the light of His love and wisdom, yet without that divine anchor, we are left feeling empty and unmoored.

In our day-to-day lives, we may achieve success, accumulate possessions, or experience fleeting moments of happiness, but these things fail to fill the deep void in our hearts. This void only finds satisfaction when we invite God into our lives, allowing His truth and grace to transform us from within. Scripture reminds us that we are created for a purpose—to reflect His glory and to live as bearers of

His love. Without this connection, our identity crumbles, and we lose sight of the destiny God has lovingly planned for us.

When we embrace His presence, our spirit is renewed and our path is illuminated with hope and purpose. In His embrace, we find that we are not defined by our circumstances, but by the unfathomable love of a God who cares deeply for us. The transformative power of His presence reclaims what was lost and empowers us to overcome every challenge. Without Him, our spirit would remain adrift, but with Him, we are firmly anchored, guided, and forever cherished.

Imagine a house built with impeccable craftsmanship, where every electrical wire is neatly installed, every appliance is hooked up, and every switch is in its proper place. Yet, if the house is not connected to a power source—be it the electrical grid or a reliable generator—it remains dark and lifeless. No matter how advanced the wiring system is, without a flow of electricity, the house functions as if it were not wired at all. In the same way, our spiritual lives need a constant, divine power supply to truly come alive and flourish.

Our spirit, much like the electrical system of a house, is designed for energy and vitality. It is meant to be activated by a continuous source of divine connection—an eternal power that sustains us every day. That ultimate power source is found at the ultimate of all altars, the place where we come into communion with God. When we remain at this sacred altar, our spirit finds solace, direction, and the energy it needs to navigate the complexities of life.

Staying connected to God is not a one-time event; it's a daily commitment. Just as a house requires an uninterrupted connection to the electrical grid to keep its lights on and its appliances running, we must consistently draw on God's presence to live fully. Without His life-giving energy, our inner selves become dim, our purpose becomes unclear, and we risk wandering through life like a house in darkness—uninspired, unproductive, and disconnected from the source of true light.

This daily communion with God is more than a ritual—it is the very act that transforms our inner being. It ignites our passion, clarifies our purpose, and strengthens our resolve to overcome challenges. At the ultimate altar, where our spirit meets the divine, we find a sanctuary that rejuvenates our souls. This sacred space is where we receive guidance, where our hearts are refreshed, and where we find the power to face each new day. It is here that the Holy Spirit fills us with the energy we need to shine our light in a world that often dwells in darkness.

Moreover, the ultimate altar symbolizes our ongoing relationship with God, a relationship that is both intimate and sustaining. It is not enough to simply build a spiritual house—our daily routines and practices must be connected to the divine source. Without that connection, even the most beautiful spiritual structures we create will remain inert, lacking the dynamic energy needed to truly impact our lives and the lives of those around us.

As believers, we are called to be more than passive recipients of grace. We are invited to actively engage in worship and communion, to consistently return to the ultimate altar where God's presence is most palpable. In doing so, we ensure that our spiritual circuits are complete and that our souls remain energized and aligned with His purpose. Just as a house lights up when connected to power, our lives radiate with purpose and joy when we remain steadfast in our connection to God.

Thus, without a steady connection to the ultimate altar—the place where our spirit finds its nourishment—we become like a house with perfect wiring but no power source. To truly come alive each day, we must continually return to that sacred space, where God's energy flows into us, guiding our steps, illuminating our path, and empowering us to fulfill the destiny He has planned for us.

Bear in mind that there is no mission more important for the devil than to sever the connection between your spirit and the spirit of God. This is his primary strategy—to isolate you from the divine presence, so that you become vulnerable to his influence. In spiritual matters, there is no void; every gap left by the absence of God is quickly filled by the enemy's schemes. When you are disconnected from the ultimate source of life, your spirit becomes an open door for the forces of darkness to enter and take hold.

Imagine your soul as a fortress built for communion with God. When every wall is strong and every gate is open to the divine, no enemy can breach your defenses. However, when you allow distractions, sin, or neglect to create a gap in that fortress, the devil moves in. He exploits even the smallest disconnect, turning what was once a place of refuge into a vulnerability. Once he manages to cut you off from

God's presence—even momentarily—he is not leaving a void; he is actively replacing it with his own influence, aligning you with his kingdom, whether you are aware of it or not.

This process is insidious. The devil does not simply let you be; he moves strategically to pull you away from the light. Every moment of spiritual isolation is an opportunity for him to plant seeds of doubt, fear, and rebellion. The enemy uses tactics such as discouragement, distraction, and deception to ensure that your focus shifts from God to the transient and often destructive things of the world. His goal is to create an environment where you no longer sense the vital, sustaining presence of God and where his own voice becomes louder in your heart.

In essence, your spiritual connection is like a lifeline. It is the channel through which God communicates, renews, and empowers you. When that connection is robust, you experience the fullness of life and truth that comes from being in His presence. But if that connection is weakened, even for a short time, the enemy seizes the opportunity to fill that void with his own counterfeit offers. These deceptive promises can seem appealing in moments of weakness, yet they are designed to lead you further away from true freedom and joy in God.

The crucial point is that the devil's strategy is not passive; it is active and relentless. His entire agenda is focused on keeping you separated from the spirit of God because he knows that without that divine connection, your identity, purpose, and power are all at risk. Therefore, maintaining an unbroken, constant communion with God is not just beneficial—it is essential for your spiritual survival. When you intentionally nurture your relationship with God through prayer, worship, and obedience, you fortify that connection against any intrusion from the enemy.

Ultimately, the battle for your spirit is ongoing, and the enemy's success depends on your willingness to remain connected to the source of all life. Every moment spent in God's presence reinforces your strength, aligns you with His kingdom, and leaves no room for the devil to insert his influence. In a world where every gap is quickly filled, ensure that the space in your heart is reserved exclusively for the life-giving presence of God.

Revelation 11:15-17 celebrates Christ's triumph:

> *"The kingdom of the world has become the kingdom of our Lord and of His Christ."*

Once Jesus declared, *"It is finished,"* His heart was set on a singular, glorious mission: to see the kingdom of the world become the kingdom of our Lord and of His Christ. His suffering and death on the cross were not in vain; they were the means by which He secured victory over sin, death, and the powers of darkness. In that climactic moment, Jesus not only completed the work of redemption but also established the blueprint for a new order—a kingdom where His love, grace, and truth reign supreme. This ultimate sacrifice was meant to usher in an era where every human heart could be transformed by His redeeming power. His declaration signified the fulfillment of God's plan for salvation and the defeat of the old order, replacing it with a kingdom founded on righteousness and eternal hope. The significance of that moment transcends history, calling each of us to embrace the reality of His victory, and to live in the assurance that the power of His sacrifice continues to resonate in every aspect of our lives today.

Even though Jesus has given us the keys to death and hell, symbolizing complete victory over darkness, our responsibility does not end there. We are called to come to the altar each day, seeking His guidance and renewing our commitment to the journey He has called us to. The keys represent authority and access—access to divine wisdom, protection, and the fullness of life in Christ. Yet, these keys are only effective when we actively stand at the door of our hearts, open to His leading. Each day, as we approach the altar in prayer and worship, we not only receive His direction but also become instruments of His grace, inviting others to experience the transformative power of His love. In doing so, we ensure that His kingdom continues to grow, as our lives radiate the light of His eternal truth and mercy."

At the altar, you gain clarity on the specific door that God has opened for you that day. In that sacred space of communion, your spirit aligns with His divine will, and you become attuned to the opportunities He lays before you. As you dwell at the altar, you learn to discern the subtle guidance of the Holy Spirit, which directs your path and prepares you to walk confidently into new realms of possibility. Remember the words of Jesus:

> So Jesus explained, "I tell you the truth, the Son can do nothing by himself. He does only what he sees the Father doing. Whatever the Father does, the Son also does.

These words remind us that true discipleship involves not only observing but also joining in the work of God. By spending time in worship and intimate prayer, you position yourself to follow Him, step by step, as He reveals which door to open each day. This ongoing connection transforms your life, making each moment an opportunity to partner with the Divine in shaping your destiny and ensuring that you are ever-ready to embrace His plans without hesitation.

Equally important is the understanding that "he that walks in the day does not stumble," yet the spiritual day remains unseen unless you continually return to the altar. Without this daily practice of communion, your spirit can drift in darkness, vulnerable to the pitfalls of uncertainty and distraction. When you remain at the altar, you not only sustain your connection to God but also empower your walk in the spiritual realm. It is here, in this intimate encounter with the Creator, that your inner light is renewed, preventing you from stumbling even when external challenges arise. In essence, the altar is your spiritual gateway—it is where divine clarity meets human resolve, ensuring that every step you take is guided by the eternal wisdom and power of God.

Questions for Reflection

1. Moses lived under the old covenant with many sacrifices for the people's sins. The new covenant was established when Jesus said at the last supper, **"This cup *is* the new covenant in My blood, which is shed for you"** (Luke 22:20, NKJV). Not long after His death and resurrection, His church was established. Are you meeting regularly with a body of believers? What can you do to serve His church? What can you do to grow His church?

2. After spending extended time with God, Moses' face radiated His glory. Are you carving time out of each day to spend in the presence of God? In what ways are you daily seeking Him? How can you share His glory with others?

3. Take some time to read the following gospel accounts of Jesus' crucifixion. Meditate on what He has done for you and write down your thoughts.

   Matthew 27:27-56; Mark 15:21-41; Luke 23:26-49; John 19:17-37

CHAPTER 11

CONCLUDING THOUGHTS

Thered is a correct way God desires to be approached, and He has set this standard in Scripture so that as children of the Kingdom, we do not run our lives by the rules of the world. The systems of the world are inherently opposed to God's ways— they exist as parallel lines that never intersect. God's instructions remind us that His way is the only path that leads to true fulfillment and eternal life. We are called to align our lives with His divine order rather than succumb to worldly principles that lead only to spiritual emptiness.

Reflecting on our early experiences in faith, many of us have witnessed the deep burden placed upon prayer meetings in churches. Whether through verbal prayer requests or written prayer slips, believers once eagerly lifted each other's burdens before the Lord. We recall the time when the church rejoiced collectively for the answered prayers, much like the church did when Peter was in prison (Acts 12:5). In those times, there was a spirit of unity and mutual support— no gossip or judgment followed as we saw genuine love and care for one another. Sadly, this atmosphere has shifted. Today, many are reluctant to share their struggles publicly for fear that their issues may become fodder for gossip or lead to unwarranted judgment. The pure, unreserved support that once characterized corporate prayer seems to have given way to a guarded approach where individuals hesitate to reveal their vulnerabilities. This shift diminishes the power of communal intercession and the transformative fellowship that arises when believers come together in heartfelt prayer.

We overcome by the blood of the Lamb and the word of our testimony (Revelation 12:11). Yet, the enemy has taken deep root in many church communities, creating an environment where safe spaces for sharing testimonies of God's great wonders are scarce. Many believers are afraid that if they share their testimonies, their stories might be dismissed, or worse, twisted to discredit the work of God in their lives. I find it baffling when I encounter people who claim to have experienced miraculous breakthroughs, only to have those very blessings later snatched away by the influence of demonic forces. This incongruity leaves me questioning: which God did they truly pray to—one who grants and sustains blessings, or one whose power is easily undermined? It raises concerns about whether they fully belong to the Kingdom that Christ came to establish.

The so-called "enemy syndrome" prevalent in many African churches is yet another tool the devil uses to draw Christians away from the true doctrines of Christ. Do not misunderstand me; if Scripture declares that "your adversary the devil walks about like a roaring lion" (1 Peter 5:8, NKJV), then indeed the devil is on the loose. However, how much more powerful is the God we serve! When we live in constant fear of what the devil might do, we forget our authority in Christ. Once we understand that God is a terror to the devil and his kingdom, we will realize that Satan must ultimately bow before the Almighty. But if we remain under the bondage of fear—failing to recognize the unlimited power of the Most High to subdue every force, be it demonic or human—then we have a serious problem in our spiritual walk.

As children of the Kingdom, we are continually being shaped into the image of Christ by consistently communing with Him at the altar. Our spirit is daily molded into the fearless, courageous, and anointed nature of the Lion of the tribe of Judah, setting us apart from the common man. When Jesus explained how Kingdom people operate, He urged us not to worry about worldly needs but to trust in God's provision. In Matthew 6:31-34, He instructs, "Therefore do not worry, saying, 'What shall we eat?' or 'What shall we drink?' or 'What shall we wear?'... But seek first the kingdom of God and his righteousness, and all these things will be added to you." His words remind us that our focus should be on pursuing God's Kingdom rather than on the transient concerns of this world.

Jesus demonstrated this principle repeatedly. When He was approached about paying the temple tax, He directed Peter to find a coin in the mouth of a fish—a miraculous act that underscored His divine provision. Similarly, when He needed a donkey, Jesus simply instructed His disciples to speak to a man, and the necessary means were provided. These examples teach us that as long as we adhere to the principles of the Kingdom, God will ensure that we are never left stranded. However, once we deviate from His path, our lives can quickly become dictated by our own desires and fears, leading us to worship anything other than God.

The true essence of Kingdom living lies in maintaining constant communion with the Lord. When we consistently meet Him at the altar—whether in private devotion or in corporate worship—we tap into a divine reservoir of strength, wisdom, and guidance. This continual engagement with God transforms our lives, allowing us to experience His peace even amidst trials. It is not merely about receiving blessings; it is about aligning our very being with His purpose. The blood of the Lamb secures our victory, and our testimony becomes a testament to His unfailing love and power.

Let us, therefore, commit to a lifestyle of fearless, unwavering devotion to God. May our daily walks be marked by an intimate connection with the Lord, a connection that empowers us to live boldly and purposefully, allowing the light of Christ to shine brightly in every corner of our lives to every corner of the world.

EPILOGUE

THE ALTAR: MEANING, SIGNIFICANCE AND CHURCH TRADITIONS

THE ALTAR AS DIVINE ENCOUNTER

The altar is more than a physical structure; it is a sacred threshold where heaven and earth intersect. From the earliest pages of Scripture to the modern practice of Christian worship, the altar has served as a symbol of covenant, sacrifice, and communion. It is a place of surrender, where humanity offers its brokenness to God, and God responds with grace, mercy, and transformation. To understand the altar is to grasp the heartbeat of biblical worship—a rhythm of giving and receiving, of death and resurrection.

This chapter lays the theological and spiritual foundation for the altar's role in Christian faith. We will explore its origins in Scripture, trace its evolution through biblical history, and examine its ultimate fulfillment in Jesus Christ. Along the way, we will engage insights from theologians, pastors, and mystics who have contemplated the altar's profound significance. By the end, readers will see that the altar is not merely a relic of ancient religion but a living reality that shapes our relationship with God today.

I. BIBLICAL ROOTS: OLD TESTAMENT FOUNDATIONS

A. Altars in the Patriarchal Era

The first altars in Scripture emerge in the stories of Noah, Abraham, Isaac, and Jacob. These primitive structures—often simple piles of uncut stones—were spaces of divine encounter. After the flood, Noah built an altar to the Lord, offering burnt sacrifices (Genesis 8:20). This act of gratitude and atonement marked humanity's renewed covenant with God.

For Abraham, altars became landmarks of faith. At Shechem, Bethel, and Hebron, he erected altars to commemorate God's promises (Genesis 12:7, 13:18). These were not merely ritualistic acts but declarations of trust. As theologian Walter Brueggemann notes, "Abraham's altars signified his readiness to stake his life on Yahweh's faithfulness." Each altar marked a step in Abraham's journey from uncertainty to covenant certainty.

Jacob's dream at Bethel (Genesis 28:10-22) further unveils the altar's significance. After encountering God in a vision of a ladder bridging heaven and earth, Jacob anoints a stone and vows, "This stone… shall be God's house" (v. 22). Here, the altar becomes a portal—a place where the divine and human realms meet.

B. The Mosaic Altar: Sacrifice and Sanctity

With the Exodus, the altar took on a more formal role in Israel's worship. God instructed Moses to construct a bronze altar for burnt offerings as part of the Tabernacle (Exodus 27:1-8). This portable altar symbolized God's presence among His people during their wilderness wanderings. The daily sacrifices—bulls, lambs, grain, and incense—were not arbitrary rituals but embodied profound truths: sin required atonement, life demanded consecration, and worship necessitated surrender.

The Levitical laws emphasized the altar's holiness. Only priests could approach it, and even then, with meticulous care (Leviticus 1–7). The blood of sacrifices, sprinkled on the altar's horns, served as a visceral reminder of sin's cost and grace's necessity. As John Calvin later reflected, "The altar was a school where Israel learned the gravity of sin and the depth of God's mercy."

C. The Temple Altar: A Dwelling Place for Glory

Solomon's Temple elevated the altar's grandeur. The bronze altar in the courtyard (2 Chronicles 4:1) and the golden altar of incense in the Holy Place (Exodus 30:1-10) became focal points of Israel's worship. The Temple itself was designed as a microcosm of creation, with the altar at its heart—a symbol of God's reign over all things.

Yet the prophets soon critiqued empty ritualism. Amos condemned those who "offer sacrifices on altars of stone" while ignoring justice (Amos 5:21-24). Isaiah called Israel to "wash and make yourselves clean" rather than rely on mechanical offerings (Isaiah 1:11-17). The altar, when divorced from repentance and righteousness, became a hollow shell.

II. THE NEW TESTAMENT FULFILLMENT: CHRIST AS ALTAR AND SACRIFICE

A. The End of All Altars

The New Testament opens with a startling claim: Jesus Christ is the "Lamb of God, who takes away the sin of the world" (John 1:29). In His life, death, and resurrection, Christ fulfilled the Old Testament sacrificial system. The book of Hebrews declares that animal sacrifices were "a shadow of the good things to come," while Christ's once-for-all offering achieved eternal redemption (Hebrews 10:1-14).

The cross became the ultimate altar. On Golgotha, Jesus offered Himself as the perfect sacrifice, "without blemish" (1 Peter 1:19). Early church fathers like Augustine saw the cross as the convergence of all prior altars: "What the blood of bulls could not accomplish, the blood of Christ accomplished forever."

B. The Altar Transformed

In Christ, the physical altar gave way to a spiritual reality. The writer of Hebrews urges believers to "offer a sacrifice of praise" (13:15) and to approach God confidently through Christ's mediation (4:16). Paul reimagines worship as the offering of one's entire life: "Present your bodies as a living sacrifice" (Romans 12:1).

This shift did not negate the altar's significance but deepened it. The early church retained the language of altar and sacrifice but applied it to the Eucharist. Ignatius of Antioch (c. 110 AD) called the communion table "the altar of God," where Christ's sacrifice is remembered and received.

III. THE ALTAR IN CHRISTIAN TRADITION

A. Early Church Perspectives

The church fathers wrestled with the altar's meaning in light of Christ. The early church fathers, navigating a world transitioning from temple worship to the radical newness of Christ's covenant, reimagined the altar not as a physical locus of ritual but as a dynamic expression of the church's identity and mission. Their reflections, forged in the crucible of persecution and theological debate, transformed the altar from a fixed stone into a living symbol of Christ's presence in His people.

Augustine of Hippo (354–430 AD), in his magnum opus *The City of God*, dismantled pagan and superficial Christian notions of sacred space. Writing in the aftermath of Rome's sack in 410 AD, he contrasted the fleeting "earthly city" with the eternal "City of God." For Augustine, the true altar was inseparable from the church itself—the Body of Christ. He argued that the church, as a communion of believers united in Christ, became the living altar where "the whole redeemed community, in union with Christ, is both the offering and the place where offering is made" (City of God, Book X). This radical shift redefined sacrifice: Christians were to offer not animals but their very lives, "a living sacrifice, holy and acceptable to God" (Romans 12:1). Augustine saw the Eucharist as the culmination of this idea, where the church, gathered at the table, both receives Christ's sacrifice and becomes "what it receives" (Sermon 272). His theology also countered the Donatist heresy, which tied sacramental efficacy to clerical purity. For Augustine, the altar's power resided not in human worthiness but in Christ's promise, making the church— flawed yet faithful—the enduring sign of God's grace.

John Chrysostom (347–407 AD), the golden-tongued preacher of Antioch and Constantinople, extended the altar's reach into everyday life. In his Homilies on Ephesians, he exhorted Christians to transform their homes into "spiritual altars" through prayer, almsgiving, and Scripture meditation. "Do you wish to see the altar of Christ?" he asked. "Take hold of the poor, for the human person is the true altar" (Homily 20 on Ephesians). Chrysostom's vision democratized holiness, urging families to practice daily worship—not in temple courts but around their tables. He linked domestic charity to the Eucharist, teaching that feeding the hungry was akin to "offering Christ Himself" on one's personal altar (Homily 50 on Matthew). This emphasis mirrored the early church's clandestine worship in homes during persecution, where the altar was wherever believers broke bread and shared life.

Origen (184–253 AD), spiritualized the altar further, interpreting it as the soul purified for divine indwelling. In Homilies on Leviticus, he wrote, "Each believer is an altar… upon which the fire of the Holy Spirit consumes worldly desires." Cyprian of Carthage (200–258 AD), amid third-century schisms, tied the altar to church unity: "There is one altar, as there is one Bishop [Christ]" (Letter 43). To Cyprian, schismatics who erected rival altars fractured the Body of Christ itself.

These perspectives birthed a tension: while post-Constantinian

Christianity built grand basilicas with marble altars, the fathers' teachings anchored the altar's essence in the community. Even as physical altars proliferated, Augustine's "City of God" reminded the church that stones were symbols, not substitutes, for the living temple of believers. Chrysostom's domestic spirituality persisted in monastic rules and later Protestant emphases on family worship.

The early church's reimagining of the altar laid the groundwork for all subsequent Christian thought. It transformed worship from a temple ritual into a holistic life of offering—where every act of love, every shared meal, and every prayer whispered in darkness became a sacrament of encounter with the God who "dwells not in temples made by hands" (Acts 17:24) but in the hearts of His people.

B. Reformation Insights

The Reformers rejected medieval notions of the altar as a place of repeated sacrifice. The Reformation of the 16th century marked a seismic shift in Christian theology, particularly in redefining the altar's role. Rejecting medieval Catholicism's understanding of the Mass as a repeated sacrifice, Reformers like Martin Luther and John Calvin recentered the altar on Christ's finished work, reshaping worship around grace, faith, and spiritual communion. Martin Luther emphasized that Christ's work was complete, declaring, "The altar is Christ; He is our priest and our offering." John Calvin, meanwhile, saw the Lord's Table as a means of grace where believers commune with Christ spiritually.

Medieval Context: The Altar as a Site of Sacrifice

In pre-Reformation Europe, the altar was the focal point of the Mass, interpreted through the lens of transubstantiation—the belief that the bread and wine became Christ's literal body and blood. The priest, acting in *persona Christi*, was seen as re-offering Christ's sacrifice to atone for sin, a practice rooted in medieval interpretations of Christ's command, "Do this in remembrance of me" (Luke 22:19). This theology, formalized at the Fourth Lateran Council (1215), framed the altar as a place where grace was "merited" through ritual. For Reformers, this undermined the sufficiency of Christ's once-for-all crucifixion (Hebrews 10:10), reducing the Eucharist to a human work rather than a divine gift.

Martin Luther (1483–1546) spearheaded the critique, declaring, "The altar is Christ; He is our priest and our offering." In *The Babylonian Captivity of the Church* (1520), he dismantled the sacrificial Mass, arguing that Christ's death was "a single, eternal sacrifice" needing no repetition. Luther's theology of justification by faith alone reframed the Eucharist as a testament to God's promise, not a priestly action. "The Mass is not a sacrifice," he wrote, "but a proclamation of Christ's victory over sin."

Luther retained a robust view of Christ's presence in the elements (consubstantiation), where Christ was present "in, with, and under" the bread and wine. Yet he rejected the altar's association with priestly power. For Luther, the priesthood of all believers (1 Peter 2:9) meant every Christian approached God through Christ, the true High Priest. Physical altars, while still used, symbolized Christ's enduring presence rather than a place of transactional sacrifice.

John Calvin (1509–1564) deepened this reimagining. In his *Institutes of the Christian Religion* (1559), he described the Lord's Supper as a "means of grace" where believers commune spiritually with the ascended Christ. Calvin rejected both transubstantiation and Luther's consubstantiation, teaching that Christ's presence was mediated by the Holy Spirit. "The Lord's Supper is a mirror," he wrote, "in which we may contemplate Christ crucified, in whom all our salvation lies."

For Calvin, the Table's purpose was not to repeat sacrifice but to nourish faith. The altar—replaced by a simple communion table—became a site of fellowship, where the church "ascends in spirit to heaven" to partake of Christ's benefits. This shift democratized worship: the Table was a gift to the congregation, not a priestly prerogative.

Legacy: From Sacrifice to Supper

The Reformation's insights transformed church architecture and practice. Altars were dismantled or replaced with wooden tables, emphasizing the Supper's communal nature. Pulpits became central, underscoring the Word's primacy alongside the sacrament. Luther and Calvin, though differing on Christ's presence, united in proclaiming the altar's fulfillment in Christ. Their teachings endure in Protestant liturgy, where the Eucharist celebrates grace received, not grace earned—a perpetual reminder that "it is finished" (John 19:30).

C. Contemporary Reflections

Modern theologians like N.T. Wright and Timothy Keller reimagine the altar not as a static relic but as a dynamic call to embody Christ's mission in the world. Wright, in The Day the Revolution Began, frames the church's vocation through the lens of sacrificial witness: "We are called to be living altars, bearing witness to Christ's reconciliation in a broken world." For Wright, the Eucharist is both a declaration of Jesus' victory and a commissioning. As believers partake, they are drawn into God's project of renewing creation— justice, mercy, and evangelism become acts of "sacrificial worship," turning Sunday's Communion into Monday's mission. The church, as a "living altar," reflects Christ's presence not only in liturgy but in feeding the hungry, advocating for the marginalized, and stewarding creation.

Timothy Keller, in Center Church, personalizes this vision, arguing that "the gospel turns every heart into an altar—a place where we die to self and rise to new life." Keller emphasizes that daily discipleship—forgiveness, humility, generosity—is where the altar's transformative power unfolds. Just as Christ's sacrifice reconciled humanity to God, believers' "living sacrifices" (Romans 12:1) reconcile communities to one another. This ethos underpins modern movements like the missional church and neo-monasticism, where shared meals, economic simplicity, and radical hospitality become expressions of "altar living."

Together, Wright and Keller bridge worship and witness, insisting that the altar's true significance lies in its overflow into the world.

The Communion table, they argue, is both a foretaste of God's kingdom and a catalyst for its coming—a reminder that every act of love, done in Christ's name, extends the altar's reach into the cracks of a fractured world.

IV. THE ALTAR'S SIGNIFICANCE TODAY

A. Personal Worship: The Altar of the Heart

The "altar within" is the intimate space where the believer meets God in daily surrender. Oswald Chambers, in My Utmost for His Highest, frames this as the crux of discipleship: "The altar is the starting place for obedience," where self-will is exchanged for divine purpose. Prayer becomes an offering of trust, repentance a laying down of sin, and Scripture reading a reception of holy instruction. This inner altar is not static but dynamic—a continual yielding, as Jesus taught: "If anyone would come after me, let him deny himself" (Luke 9:23). Here, the mundane becomes sacred; work, relationships, and suffering are transformed into "spiritual sacrifices" (1 Peter 2:5).

B. Communal Worship: The Church's Altar

The church's altar—whether a Communion table or a gathered circle—embodies unity. As "a royal priesthood" (1 Peter 2:9), the church collectively approaches God, transcending individualism. Dietrich Bonhoeffer noted, "The physical presence of others is a grace," and the altar symbolizes this shared identity. In Communion, prayer, or song, differences dissolve; the body of Christ becomes "one bread, one body" (1 Corinthians 10:17). The altar is both a reminder of Christ's reconciling work and a call to live as a reconciled people.

C. The Eucharist: Communion on the Altar

The Eucharist weaves personal devotion and communal unity into cosmic renewal. Alexander Schmemann, in For the Life of the World, calls it "the journey to the altar of the Kingdom"—a feast proclaiming Christ's past sacrifice, present nourishment, and future restoration. As bread and wine are shared, creation itself is rehallowed, and the church tastes the "already and not yet" of God's reign. Here, the altar is no longer a place but a promise: "Until He comes" (1 Corinthians 11:26).

Preparing the Altar of the Heart

The altar, transcending stone, wood, or gold, exists wherever humanity meets the divine in vulnerability and surrender. From Abraham's crude cairns to Solomon's gilded temple, from the cross of Calvary to the communion tables of today, the altar has always been a threshold—a place where God's grace interrupts human striving. As we journey through this book, we will trace how Communion, as the culmination of the altar's ancient legacy, invites us not only to remember Christ's sacrifice but to participate in its transformative power. This sacrament, as Alexander Schmemann writes, is "the journey to the altar of the Kingdom," where past, present, and future converge. Here, the fragmented pieces of our lives—our joys, sins, and hopes—are gathered up, blessed, and remade in the fire of God's love.

To approach this mystery is to embrace the paradox that we bring nothing, yet offer everything. Augustine's vision of the church as the "true altar" challenges us to see ourselves as both priests and offerings, our lives a liturgy of reconciliation in a fractured world. Yet this begins inwardly, as Timothy Keller notes, with the gospel turning "every heart into an altar," where self is crucified and Christ's life rises in its place. Personal repentance and communal worship become twin flames on the altar of the heart, igniting a holiness that spills into the mundane.

Let us, then, approach with awe—not of a distant deity, but of the God who bends near. With gratitude—for grace that turns our poverty into abundance. With readiness—to be broken like bread and poured out like wine. For in Communion, the altar is no longer a place we visit, but the people we become.

Bibliography

Brueggemann, Walter. *Genesis: A Bible Commentary for Teaching and Preaching*.

Calvin, John. *Institutes of the Christian Religion*, Book IV

Wright, N.T. *The Day the Revolution Began*.

Keller, Timothy. *The Prodigal God*.

Chambers, Oswald. My Utmost for His Highest.

Bonhoeffer, Dietrich. *Life Together*.

Schmemann, Alexander. *For the Life of the World*.

Keller, Timothy. *Center Church*.

Luther, Martin. *The Babylonian Captivity of the Church*.

The Council of Trent (1545–1563), Session XXII (Counter-Reformation response).

Augustine. *The City of God*, Book X; Sermon 272.

John Chrysostom. *Homilies on Ephesians; Homily 50 on Matthew*.

Origen. *Homilies on Leviticus*.

Cyprian. *Letter 43: To the Lapsed*.

STEPHEN OWOLABI

Made in the USA
Monee, IL
21 May 2025

17681041R00108